Tom Clancy's
RAINBOW SIX™

PRIMA PUBLISHING

Rocklin, California

(916) 632-4400

www.primagames.com

Important:
Prima Publishing has made every effort to determine that the information contained in this book is
accurate. However, the publisher makes no warranty, either expressed or implied, as to the accuracy, effectiveness, or completeness of the material in this book; nor does the publisher assume liability for damages, either incidental or consequential, that may result from using the information in
this book. The publisher cannot provide information regarding game play, hints and strategies, or
problems with hardware or software. Questions should be directed to the support numbers provided by the game and device manufacturers in their documentation. Some game tricks require precise
timing and may require repeated attempts before the desired result is achieved.

ISBN: 7615-2064-3
Library of Congress Catalog Card Number: 99-70033
Printed in the United States of America

99 0001 02 BB 10 9 8 7

ACKNOWLEDGEMENTS

I'd like to thank Carson Brice at Red Storm Entertainment. Her support helped make this project a pleasure. Thanks, also, to Doug Littlejohns for his foreword. I'd also like to acknowledge Amy Raynor and Richard Dal Porto at Prima Publishing for helping to make this book a reality.

Thanks, too, to Tom Clancy for over a decade of enjoyment through his novels and now his computer games. I have eagerly awaited every title and *Rainbow Six,* both game and novel, has lived up to all my expectations.

Finally, I thank and express my love for my wife, Trisa, who willingly sacrificed my attention during the last few weeks of her pregnancy so I could write this book, something I'd wanted to do since the game was first announced.

DEDICATION

For my beautiful new daughter, Sarah Leigh Ann Knight, who was born as this book was preparing to go to print. May you be a heavenly sunbeam in this world of shadows and darkness.

TABLE OF CONTENTS

PART 1

ORIGINAL *RAINBOW SIX* xii

PART 2

RAINBOW SIX MISSION PACK: EAGLE WATCH 172

Chapter Ten: Multiplayer Additions . . . 210

Appendix A: Roster of Operatives 214

Index 215

FOREWORD

In early October 1996, 18 about-to-be Red Storm Founder Members, myself, and Tom Clancy met in Colonial Williamsburg, Virginia for a weekend to get to know each other, have a lot of fun, discuss where we wanted to take Red Storm Entertainment, and brainstorm potential products. Tom's baseball team, the Orioles, were in the play-offs that fall, but he was so engrossed in the excitement that the meeting generated that he ignored the TV while we were talking.

We stopped the brainstorm when we had reached nearly 100 titles and started to focus on what we thought the market wanted and what we could achieve with the scant resources available to the fledgling company. Out of this came four game ideas and one was a "sort of hostage rescue game." Thus was born Rainbow Six.

After several weeks of design work we had a basis to start on the product in late November. The early team was only four strong, and it was obvious that we needed more people. Fortunately for us, along came Carl Schnurr as the producer, capital from Pearson plc., and some excellent responses to our recruiting advertisements. But it was not until about July 1997 that we were really able to open the throttle and start full development.

I would like to take the opportunity here to express my thanks and admiration to the dedicated team that made this all possible. They have coped with the ups and downs of development with unfailing good humor, they have never given up, and they are some of the finest people I have met since moving to the USA from the UK some two years ago. They roundly deserve the acclaim that I expect to be forthcoming in the next few months.

Tom was involved with the game from that first meeting. He fed in brilliant insights to the developing back story and was able to put us in touch with a cohort of experts who had done this for real. Then, during one of his regular visits to Red Storm, he

announced that his next book was going to be about antiterrorism and it was an obvious move to make sure that we stayed close to Tom as he developed his ideas and, where applicable, align the game with them.

We kicked around a number of titles, and Tom came up with this: RAINBOW is the secret international organization set up by governments to have a ready response team to deal with potentially explosive incidents. There surely is a need for such an organization, and it may already exist. However, looking back at the most recent outrage in Peru, it would seem that neither Peru nor Japan is party to any such agreement. John Clark, as the head of the organization, would have the short title of Six. Hence Rainbow Six.

This is a gripping plot, one that could happen at any time, and we have tried to ensure that it is as realistic as possible.

With the aid of this excellent guide, your mission is to "Save the World." Good luck. We are all depending on you.

Doug Littlejohns
CEO & President, Red Storm Entertainment

INTRODUCTION

Mr. Clark Returns

Tom Clancy, master of the techno-thriller, has written numerous best-selling novels. His first few dealt with the Cold War and tensions between East and West, but as relations thawed Clancy evolved and he continues writing frighteningly realistic, relevant novels.

Global nuclear holocaust may seem less likely to us than it once did, but far more sinister dangers lurk in today's shadows. ICBMs have been replaced by small nuclear devices–"suitcase nukes"–anyone could carry from one country into another. Chemical and biological weapons can cause as much death as a world war.

Terrorism is the new threat to world peace. Large-scale warfare is too expensive for all but a handful of countries. But a rogue nation could bring a superpower to its knees using only a few people armed with these weapons of mass destruction. Such weapons became more available with the collapse of the Soviet Union and the ensuing instability. Now, powerful and deadly weapons are available to the highest bidder, whether small country, disaffected group, or business corporation.

One needn't look far to find terrorism. As this book goes to print, real-world terrorists have just bombed U.S. embassies in Kenya and Tanzania. The need exists for an international antiterrorist team: RAINBOW may exist. We'd never know.

Although board games and computer simulations have been designed based on Clancy novels, including *The Hunt for Red October* and *Red Storm Rising*, they don't approach the level of *Rainbow Six*. Novel and game go hand-in-hand, involving the reader in the game and the player in the book.

How to Use This Guide

This guide will help you become an efficient soldier in the war against terrorism. *Rainbow Six* is unlike any game you've played before. You must combine strategy, tactics, and eye-hand coordi-

nation to make your way through to the game's climactic finale. Because you're probably not expert in the techniques of antiterrorism and hostage rescue, this book takes you step-by-step, giving you the information you need to lead RAINBOW to victory.

The first chapter covers the skills you need to progress through the game. It includes tutorials where you can practice what you learn. Chapter 2 provides dossiers on each RAINBOW operative, as well as important information on how to use them. RAINBOW provides an arsenal of weapons and equipment for battling terrorists; Chapter 3 goes over each item you can carry and how to use it best. The fourth chapter discusses tactics for completing your missions. It includes more tutorials to help you reach the operational level necessary to tackle the campaign.

You can't just run through a mission, blowing everyone away single-handedly. You must organize various operatives into teams. To have each do what must be done, you must plan each mission in detail. Chapter 5 gives you the plan on planning. Next, Chapter 6 provides strategies, tactics, and maps for each of the campaign's 16 missions.

Finally, Chapter 7 covers the game's extensive multiplayer capability, providing tips for working with other players, as well as for defeating them.

Section 2 of this book (starting with Chapter 8) covers the Eagle Watch Mission Pack. This addition begins where the original game left off. Terrorists are continuing their hostile actions against innocents. This time, they have chosen some exotic locations as well as one close to home. The four new operatives and the new weapons are covered in Chapter 8. The Mission Pack includes five new and challenging missions. Chapter 9 helps you plan effective and successful strategies and tactics to accomplish each of the new missions with no loss of life to your team or the hostages it must rescue.

Chapter 10 covers the new types of multiplayer games in the Mission Pack as well as tips for each of the new maps. Finally, Appendix A provides a list of all operatives on the Rainbow team, and their skill levels from both the original game and the Eagle Watch Mission Pack.

Tom Clancy's RAINBOW SIX

ORIGINAL RAINBOW SIX

PART 1

Tom Clancy's
RAINBOW SIX™

CHAPTER ONE
BASIC TRAINING

Controlling the Characters

During any mission, you control one team member directly. The others rely on orders you issue during the planning phase. (Chapter 5 covers planning in detail.)

Control breaks down into movement and weapons. In combat, you must handle both smoothly and simultaneously. To achieve this, first master them individually and then put them together.

Movement

In *Rainbow Six* you may choose how to control your team members during a mission. Using the numeric keypad allows you to move forward and backward and turn in both directions. Hold down Ⓢ as you turn to strafe left or right. This is similar to controls in some first-person shooter games, and you may feel most comfortable with it. I recommend the second, more advanced method, however, using mouse and keyboard together. This may take getting used to, but it's far superior to the first method.

The advanced control uses the arrow keys to move forward and backward and strafe left and right. The mouse controls the direction your character faces, as well as the elevation of his or her line of sight. Move the mouse forward to look up and back to look down, for example. Left and right motions turn your character in the corresponding direction. Press the right-hand mouse button to run as you move forward.

To crouch to avoid exposure, press END. Press 0 on the keypad to manipulate your environment–open doors, climb ladders, surmount obstacles, and the like. You may have noticed that "jump" is missing. This is intentional. Jumping is an uncontrolled movement: once you're in the air, you can't stop or change direction until your feet hit the ground again. Teams such as Rainbow avoid uncontrolled movement. Their missions are difficult and deadly enough without further variables. Besides, none of the training exercises or missions require jumping.

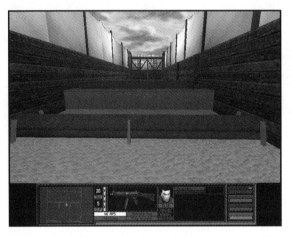

Fig. 1-1. The Obstacle Course tests your ability to control a character.

The Obstacle Course

To practice what you've learned about movement, select Training from the main menu. Under Fire and Movement, highlight Obstacle Course, and then click Start Tutorial. You'll get control of Rainbow team member Ding Chavez, and begin at one end of the course. Press F1 to toggle between first- and third person views. For this exercise, you'll use third-person.

The maze lies straight ahead. The lower-right corner of the screen displays a minimap of your surroundings. Press [or] to zoom in and out, and M for a full-screen view of the map. Press M again to return to action view. Using the mouse to "steer," press the arrow keys to move through the maze to the end.

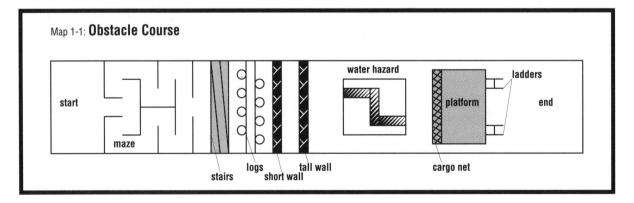

Map 1-1: **Obstacle Course**

When you exit the maze, you'll come to a short flight of stairs. Climb up and walk off the end to fall back to the ground. The next obstacle is a pair of logs: holding down the right mouse button, run forward to clear the logs easily. Next, you face a pair of walls, the first short and the other of medium height. Move close to the first and press keypad [0]. Chavez will climb to the top. Walk off the other edge and repeat at the next wall.

Now, carefully cross the wood planks over the water hazard. This is good practice for negotiating ledges and other narrow paths. Try this looking down and straight ahead, in both first- and third-person views. If you fall off, move to the water's edge and press [0] to climb out.

Fig. 1-2. The water hazard requires careful footwork.

Your final obstacle is the climbing platform. Move close to the cargo net and press [0] to climb. Press the arrow key as if you were moving forward to continue to the top. Hold down the right-hand mouse button to climb more quickly. At the top, move across the platform to a ladder. Press [0] again to climb down.

Congratulations! You've completed the Obstacle Course and are ready for weapons training.

Firearms

Moving can be fun, but this game is about combat. The weapons in *Rainbow Six* are realistically modeled after weapons antiterrorist groups actually use. Chapter 3 covers weapons in greater detail. Before heading out to the Shooting Range, read over the following paragraphs.

You practiced advanced control earlier, and you'll use it again. During the Obstacle Course exercise, a targeting reticle (a circle with four lines extending in the four compass directions) was always in the center of your view. The reticle shows you where your rounds probably will hit. Although the circle remains the same, the four short lines move out from the

Fig. 1-3. At the climbing platform you must climb up a cargo net and down a ladder.

circle, reflecting the area where your bullets will strike, as accuracy changes. You want to keep this area as small as possible.

Factors affecting accuracy include fatigue, health, distractions, and taking hits. As your character becomes tired or wounded, his or her accuracy decreases permanently for the rest of the mission. Distractions such as flashbangs, seeing a teammate or hostage go down, or hearing an alarm go off decrease accuracy temporarily.

To fire a gun, click the left mouse button. You may select a rate of fire—that is, the number of rounds fired each time you click the mouse—for any gun. Each gun has a safety and single-shot setting. When the safety is on, the weapon won't fire. The single-shot setting fires one round each time you pull the trigger (click on the mouse). Submachine guns and rifles have two additional settings—three-round burst and full-automatic. The first fires three rounds and stops each time you click on the mouse. Full-automatic continues firing as long as you hold the fire button down until the clip is empty. To change a weapon's rate of fire, press [.] on the keypad.

Each firearm affords its own level of accuracy. A pistol is less accurate than a rifle, largely because of its shorter barrel. Rate of fire affects accuracy, as well. For example, firing at full-automatic, the first few rounds probably will hit the target, but the remaining rounds will scatter. This is the main reason for the three-round burst setting: Studies show accuracy decreases dramatically after firing three rounds. When a gun fires once, its recoil alters a weapon's aim just a bit. The effects of multiple recoils in a short amount of time during full-automatic firing can change the aim significantly. Any round that doesn't hit its target is wasted. All rounds of a three-round burst should hit the target, and then allow the shooter to correct the aim and fire again. Full-automatic is suited only for spraying a lot of bullets into an area when accuracy and ammunition aren't concerns. Remember, a round that misses its target will hit *something*. Take care that hostages and other team members aren't on the receiving end of your stray bullets.

Tip

The three-round burst is the best rate of fire during missions. It's nearly as accurate as single-shot, yet packs a punch that will knock the target down. Use full-automatic only when you want to hose down an area with lead and you have ammunition to spare.

A shooter's motion also affects accuracy. When a person is walking, it's harder to keep a firearm trained on a target. Running increases the difficulty. When you move, the gun tends to move up and down and side to side along with your body. You'll notice how forward and backward motion affect accuracy, but it's turning that really decreases it. If possible, avoid turning and try to sidestep when you fire.

Fig. 1-4. Three team members improve their firearms skills at the Shooting Range—not a welcome sight for a terrorist.

Shooting Range

You can practice using all firearms in the *Rainbow Six* arsenal from all ranges at the Shooting Range. Select Shooting Range I from the training menu to go there. Your character will be armed with an HKMP5-A2, the best weapon available and extremely accurate.

Walk toward the short range and up to the counter. To change the weapon's rate of fire, press keypad $\boxed{.}$. Choose full-automatic, take aim at a target, and empty the clip. Most rounds should strike the target, but you can see how they spread. Press $\boxed{\text{DELETE}}$ to load a second clip. Changing a magazine in *Rainbow Six* takes time, just as it does in real life. Select single-shot and fire six rounds at another target. Notice that

Fig. 1-5. Practice moving fire at the walk-up exercise area.

they're close together, with little spread. Finally, fire the remainder of the clip at the third target using three-round bursts. You'll notice the groupings are very close together—much better than on full-automatic.

Reload and move to the walk-up range. Here you'll shoot at the black target as you walk along the short gravel path, both to practice shooting on the move and to see how such movement affects your accuracy. Press [2] on the regular keyboard to pull out your pistol and repeat the walk-up shooting exercise. You'll find the pistol isn't as accurate. Try it out at the short range, too.

Next, move on to the medium range and try both weapons. For a better view of your targets and where your rounds hit, press [CTRL] to activate Sniper mode. This zooms in the view. You should discover that your accuracy decreases as range increases, especially when you fire at full-automatic. Do the same at the long range.

After experimenting with the HKMP5-A2, exit the shooting range and load the Shooting Range II tutorial. It's the same range, but now your character uses a CAR-15. This is a better weapon for shooting at long range, but take care using it at full-automatic. It tends to spread bullets all over the place—bad if hostages or other team members are near your target. You can get to the shooting range under Open Training at the Training menu, as well. With this, you can choose any team member and load them out with the weapons of your choice for additional practice.

Fig. 1-6. You may need to use the Sniper view when firing at the long range, both to see where your shots hit and for targeting.

Breaching

Most of *Rainbow Six*'s missions involve combat in urban environments, and nearly all require your teams to enter buildings. In this section, you'll learn how to enter buildings using breaching devices and explosives. Your mother may have taught you to knock, but antiterrorist tactics require you to open the doors for yourself.

When you confront a closed door, you must choose how you want to open it. To open a door normally, walk over to it and press keypad $\boxed{0}$. Normally it takes a few seconds to open. If it takes a lot longer, it's locked. If silence is key to a mission, let your character pick the lock. You do this the same way you open the door; it just takes a lot longer. A lockpick kit, either your character's or another team member's, will shorten the time it takes to pick a lock.

When stealth isn't a factor, you have more choices. Blasting a door's lock with a shotgun will open it easily. Or try a door charge. This involves placing small amounts of explosives around a door, and then detonating them to blow it in, removing the door from your path and stunning the room's occupants for a moment. To use a door charge, select it as your active item. Move to a door and click the mouse. It takes time to place the charge. Step back a bit and click the mouse again to detonate it. Quickly switch back to a gun before running into the room.

Fig. 1-7. A few shotgun blasts will blow in most locked doors.

Door Breaching

Select Door Breaching from the Training menu to go to the Demolitions Range. Your character will be armed with a shotgun and some breaching charges. Walk to the Breaching Room and stand next to the door on the right. Press keypad 0. The door is locked, so hold down the key until it opens. It would have taken less time if you'd had a lockpick kit.

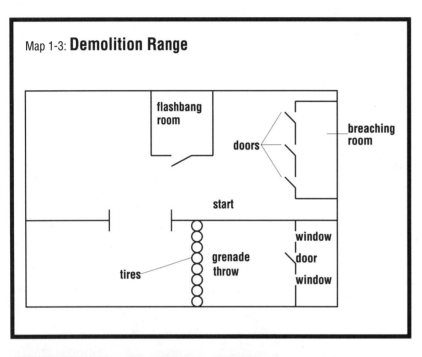

Sidestep to the center door and aim the shotgun at the lock. Fire until it blows open. You've just performed a shotgun breach. Now position your character in front of the last locked door. Press keyboard 3 to select the breaching charge, and hold down the left mouse button to place it. Now back away from the door and click the mouse again. This detonates the charge, blasting the door out of your way. The breaching charge also acts like a flashbang to those on the other side of the door.

Fig. 1-8. The breaching charge is ready to detonate. The explosion blasts the door in and stuns the room's occupants.

Place the other breaching charge on the door to the flashbang room. Then switch back to the shotgun or pistol. You needn't detonate the charge right away. When you're ready, make the charge your active item and click the mouse to detonate it. You can practice more breaching, including using the lockpick, at the Demolitions Range under Open Training.

Grenades

Grenades can help significantly when it comes to entering a
room or building safely. Rainbow operatives have two types at
their disposal–flashbangs and fragmentation grenades.
Flashbangs explode with a loud noise and a bright flash of
light. They're also called stun grenades, because this briefly
stuns persons nearby. The effect lasts only a few seconds, but
this can be long enough for your team to enter a room and kill
all the terrorists within.

Fragmentation grenades are those the military uses in combat. When they explode, they send shards of shrapnel flying in
all directions, killing those close by and wounding others farther away. Take care when using fragmentation grenades; their
blast radius may be greater than the distance your character can
throw them. Make sure you have some cover to hide behind
after you throw one.

Grenade Practice

This exercise takes place on the Demolition Range.
First, walk to the flashbang room and open the
door any way you choose. Press keyboard 3 to
make flashbangs your current item. Aim the reticle
at the door and press the mouse button. Release it
to throw. The longer you hold down the button,
the farther you'll throw the grenade. If you're too
close to the flashbang when it goes off, the screen
will go black briefly: you've stunned yourself. Back
away from the door or sidestep after throwing to
avoid the blast. After a few tries, try running into
the room after the grenade goes off without being stunned.

Fig. 1-9. Throw the flashbang through
the doorway. Don't stand too close, or
you'll end up stunning yourself.

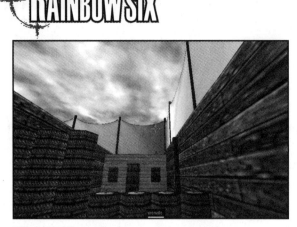

Fig. 1-10. Throw the fragmentation grenades over the tires, or you'll kill your character. Practice throwing grenades through the doorway as well as the windows.

Fig. 1-11. Hide behind the crates as you move up the street.

Fig. 1-12. These are only pop-up targets. If they were real terrorists, you'd be in a lot of trouble if you didn't take them down quickly.

Now walk to the grenade-throwing area, near the stacked tires. Many first-time grenade-users stand right next to the tires. Often the grenade will hit the tires, fall next to your character, and kill him or her. Instead, back away from the tires a bit. Throw a flashbang or two over the tires before trying a fragmentation grenade. Move the reticle up and down to adjust your throwing angle. Throw a fragmentation grenade through the door of the mock building. If you're really good, try throwing a grenade through each window. For more practice using grenades, go to the Demolitions Range under Open Training.

Additional Practice

You've practiced shooting at stationary targets as you lean on a counter. It's time to advance to the next level. This section includes one more training exercise to give you the experience you'll need to progress to exercises where you face opposition.

Fire and Movement

The final training exercise involves both fire and movement. You must advance down a mock city street, taking out pop-up targets in the windows. Although you could move out into the open, practice using cover.

In the middle of the street are several piles of crates. Run to the first and crouch. Shoot as many targets as you can from there. Slowly move out from behind the crates to take out the remainder. Run to the next stack and repeat. Continue toward the building at the end of the exercise area, where twelve targets will pop out all at once. During this exercise, practice using single-shot, three-round burst, and full-automatic.

Rainbow Six puts you in command of a team of 20 operatives from around the world. Each has unique strengths and weaknesses. It's up to you to assign them roles that maximize their skills. This chapter covers each Rainbow Six team member, providing background, personal information, attributes, and suggestions for how best to use him or her during operational missions.

Attributes

Attributes fall into two categories, profile and skill. The first five stats are considered profiles. These are inherent or learned attributes that demonstrate psychological make-up and physical endurance. Skills, on the other hand, are learned attributes that relate to using equipment, or to movement.

- **Aggression:** A character's basic nature. Comes into play only when a character "snaps," or loses self-control. An aggressive character may use extreme force when he or she snaps, endangering hostages and teammates alike. In similar circumstances, a passive character may freeze, or panic and run away.

- **Leadership:** Teamwork and self-control attributes. A leader with a low leadership rating reduces the values of those under his or her command. The higher the value, the better the bonus. Leadership applies whether the team leader is player or computer controlled.

- **Self-Control:** Likelihood that a nonplayer character will snap during combat. Once a character snaps, his or her aggression level determines the outcome.

- **Stamina:** How many wounds it takes to incapacitate a character. This attribute also affects fatigue levels at the end of a mission.

- **Teamwork:** How well a character works with other team members. Characters with low teamwork ratings tend to act alone; those with higher ratings will wait for teammates before entering a building or room and support others with cover fire.

- **Demolitions:** How long it takes a character to place a demo charge or disarm a bomb, and how many shots it takes to breach a locked door with a shotgun. High demolition value means quicker time and fewer shotgun blasts.

- **Electronics:** Time it takes a character to place bugs, pick locks, bypass security systems, and splice video.

- **Firearms:** Character's base accuracy with all weapons, and how actions such as movement and firing affect it.

- **Grenades:** Character's fragmentation grenade and flashbang accuracy and throwing time.

- **Stealth:** How much noise a character makes as he or she moves. The higher the value, the quieter the character. Those with low stealth values can be heard even walking slowly on normally quiet surfaces.

Specialties

Each character has a specialty—an area of expertise reflecting additional training and experience—and shows values for related attributes.

- **Assault:** Characters with the assault specialty have good firearms values. Use them for taking out terrorists and other combat actions.

- **Demolitions:** Characters with this specialty are great for breaching doors and creating access for teammates. Use them for defusing bombs and other explosives, as well. They have high demolitions and grenade values.

- **Electronics:** Electronics specialists are trained to plant bugs, deactivate security systems, and the like. Keep them out of firefights whenever possible: only two characters have this specialty.

- **Recon:** Use recon characters for surveillance and scouting. Their job is to locate the enemy without being detected, so their stealth values are high. They usually have high firearms values, as well, but keep them out of the fray when you can.

- **Command:** Only Ding Chavez has this specialty, and he has the highest possible leadership value. He should lead not only his team, but the entire mission. Members of his team have significantly increased self-control and teamwork values.

Arnavisca, Santiago

Personal Information

Identification Number: RCT0031-A1044
Nationality: Spanish
Specialty: Assault
Date of Birth: 01 January 1966
Height: 186 cm
Weight: 81 kg
Hair: Brown
Eyes: Brown
Gender: Male

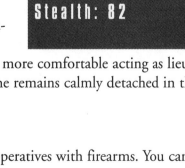

Background

Born in Malaga, Spain. Although the family's holdings shrink considerably under Franco's rule, the Arnaviscas still control large tracts of farmland around Cordoba and the Guadalquivir River valley. The second in a family of eight, his elder brother is a deputy in the Adalucian parliament. Attended University of Seville, 1983-88. Joined the *Guardia Civil* after graduation. Brigade commander 1994-96 in the Western European Union (WEU) administration of Mostar in Bosnia, where he was instrumental in rebuilding the local police force. *Guardia Civil's* counterterrorism unit, the *Unidad Especial de Intervencion* (UEI) recruited him in 1997 as part of its focus on the growing threat of terrorism within the European Union by former citizens of Yugoslavia.

Arnavisca is an expert marksman, having participated in shooting competitions since childhood. In addition to his native Spanish, he speaks English, German, and Italian fluently and can make himself understood in most other European languages. Despite his aristocratic bearing, he is more comfortable acting as lieutenant and advisor than team lead. Tenacious in combat, he remains calmly detached in the tensest situations.

Attributes

Aggression: 72
Leadership: 81
Self-control: 94
Stamina: 83
Teamwork: 92
Demolitions: 24
Electronics: 34
Firearms: 100
Grenades: 65
Stealth: 82

Notes

Arnavisca is a superb marksman and one of the two best operatives with firearms. You can use him as team leader in a pinch, but he serves far better in a supporting role. He stays cool during the hottest firefights. Arnavisca is perfect to include in the team under player control.

Beckenbauer, Lars

Personal Information

Identification Number: RCT0031-A1044
Nationality: German
Specialty: Demolitions
Date of Birth: 21 August 1953
Height: 176 cm
Weight: 87 kg
Hair: Blond
Eyes: Brown
Gender: Male

Attributes

Aggression: 55
Leadership: 78
Self-control: 77
Stamina: 81
Teamwork: 74
Demolitions: 100
Electronics: 91
Firearms: 76
Grenades: 80
Stealth: 72

Background

Born on a farm near Chemnitz on the Czechoslovakian border in then German Democratic Republic (East Germany). Drafted into the East Germany Army, 1970. Specialized in bomb disposal and demolitions. Assigned to East German Border Patrol, 1971-76. Arrested by the GDR State Security Service (Stasi) in 1976 under suspicion of involvement in high-profile defections. Released for lack of evidence and discharged from the army in 1977. Movements and activities from 1977-84 unknown. The current German government will neither confirm nor deny rumors that he was a member of the *Libellen,* an underground group responsible for bombings of East German governmental offices in and around Berlin in the summer of 1981. Resurfaced in 1985 and granted asylum by West Germany after a risky crossing of the Baltic Sea in a small sailboat. Opened Pyrotechno GmbH, a security consulting firm, in 1989. Since then, he has acquired a reputation as Germany's leading expert on explosives and demolitions. Married, 1995. Two children.

Beckenbauer has an encyclopedic knowledge of explosive devices. His years of working with bombs make him extremely meticulous. He overlooks no detail and leaves nothing to chance. Because he focuses completely on the job at hand and considers personal interactions dangerous distractions, the rest of the team may perceive him as cold and distant.

Notes

Bechenbauer is Rainbow Six's demolitions expert, and is proficient in electronics, as well. His other attributes are normal or lower. He is no leader and prefers to work alone. Put him in a team that has a strong leader and which will engage in minimal combat.

Bogart, Daniel

Personal Information

Identification Number: RCT0047-A1109
Nationality: American
Specialty: Assault
Date of Birth: 12 October 1954
Height: 188 cm
Weight: 82 kg
Hair: Black
Eyes: Brown
Gender: Male

Background

Born in Keokuk, Iowa, USA. Father is a local deputy sheriff, mother a homemaker. Two brothers. Attended University of Iowa on a track and field scholarship, 1972-76. Graduated with honors with a degree in law enforcement. Patrolman with Keokuk Police Department for three years. Hired in 1980 by the Federal Bureau of Investigation. Member, FBI Hostage Rescue Team, 1987-97. Married, 1979. Wife and two teen-age children live in Maine, USA.

Bogart makes an excellent team leader. He has exceptional tactical skills and situational awareness from his years with HRT. Cool under fire, he is a crack shot, and won marksmanship awards during his tenure at the FBI. His low-key demeanor and laconic sense of humor make him well-liked among RAINBOW team members.

Attributes

Aggression: 89
Leadership: 96
Self-control: 93
Stamina: 97
Teamwork: 95
Demolitions: 20
Electronics: 20
Firearms: 98
Grenades: 50
Stealth: 73

Notes

Bogart is a good choice for team leader. He is highly proficient with firearms, as well. Use him for your main assault teams.

Burke, Andrew

Personal Information

Identification Number: RCT0049-A2267
Nationality: British
Specialty: Assault
Date of Birth: 12 January 1968
Height: 176 cm
Weight: 72 kg
Hair: Brown
Eyes: Brown
Gender: Male

Attributes

Aggression: 91
Leadership: 85
Self-control: 75
Stamina: 94
Teamwork: 89
Demolitions: 75
Electronics: 53
Firearms: 93
Grenades: 67
Stealth: 78

Background

Born in Manchester, England. Whereabouts of father unknown. Mother is a secretary at a plastics processing plant in Leeds. Three siblings—two brothers and a sister. Joined Royal Marines, 1986. Two tours with British Special Air Service (SAS), 1989-91 and 1996-99. Received Military Cross, 1998. Has taken part in SAS actions in 22 countries on four continents. Further service record details are sealed. Unmarried.

Burke is a seasoned veteran of numerous covert operations. Although not reckless, he has a strong can-do attitude and confidence in his abilities. As a leader, he is decisive and demanding. He has a quick sense of humor and often uses jokes to relax his team before a mission. He maintains contact with his immediate family, but he considers the service to be his home.

Notes

Burke is a well-rounded operative. He has experience in most areas, but excels in none. A poor choice for team leader, he serves well in a support role for assault or other teams needing his firearms skills.

Chavez, Ding

Personal Information

Identification Number: RCT0047-X0566
Nationality: American
Specialty: Command
Date of Birth: 12 January 1968
Height: 176 cm
Weight: 72 kg
Hair: Black
Eyes: Brown
Gender: Male

Background

Born in Los Angeles, California, USA. Joined U.S. Army, 1983. Served with the 7th Infantry Division (Light), 1984-87. Achieved rank of staff sergeant before the American Central Intelligence Agency (CIA) recruited him in 1987 for narcotics interdiction operations in South America. Discharged, 1988; became a full-time CIA employee under John Clark the same year. Service records for years 1989-99 are sealed. Earned B.S. degree in political science, George Mason University, 1995. M.A., international relations, from the same institution, 1999. Married.

Chavez is an excellent light infantry soldier with an exceptional grasp of small-unit tactics and close-quarters battle. Although small in stature, he is powerfully built and agile, a formidable opponent with a wide range of weapons and in hand-to-hand combat.

Attributes

Aggression: 95
Leadership: 100
Self-control: 92
Stamina: 97
Teamwork: 94
Demolitions: 71
Electronics: 67
Firearms: 100
Grenades: 74
Stealth: 100

Notes

Chavez is operational leader of Rainbow Six. Put him in command of the team with the most important objectives. He is expert at firearms and stealth, with good experience in several other areas. His high leadership value boosts other team members with lower self-control and teamwork attributes. Put less-experienced operatives in his team. You will probably want to control Chavez, but, because he will follow your orders better than anyone else, you should leave him under AI control.

DuBarry, Alain

Personal Information

Identification Number: RCT0013-A5436
Nationality: French
Specialty: Electronics
Date of Birth: 27 September 1967
Height: 174 cm
Weight: 66 kg
Hair: Black
Eyes: Brown
Gender: Male

Attributes

Aggression: 72
Leadership: 81
Self-control: 76
Stamina: 91
Teamwork: 66
Demolitions: 76
Electronics: 100
Firearms: 84
Grenades: 81
Stealth: 73

Background

Born in Chantilly, France. Father is manuscript curator at a local museum, mother a journalist. Four sisters, two brothers. Second-oldest sister is a prominent professor of mathematics at the University of Paris. Attended *l'fcole Superieure d'Ingenieurs en Electrotechnique et Electronique* (ESIEE) in Paris, 1984-89. Graduated with degrees in electronics engineering and computer science. Joined the *Gendarmerie Nationale* in 1990 as an officer in their computer crime division. Instrumental in thwarting a 1994 attempt by Algerian nationals to bring down the French Minitel computer network using a virus spread by telephone switching software. *Groupe d'Intervention Gendarmerie Nationale* (GIGN), France's elite counterterrorist unit, recruited him in 1996 as a specialist in telephony and electronic surveillance. Unmarried.

DuBarry is expert in computers and computer nets, and in more conventional forms of surveillance. Although his role in CT actions is usually intelligence-gathering and communications, as a veteran of GIGN's extensive combat training, he is fully qualified to participate in armed operations. Introverted, thoughtful, and an excellent tactician, he often makes connections other team members miss. Off duty, he is an avid amateur scuba diver and an officer in the *Confederation Mondiale des Activites Subaquatiques* (CMAS).

Notes

DuBarry is Rainbow Six's electronics expert. He's proficient in the use of firearms and grenades, as well. He'll do well in a team with a good leader. Keep him out of combat when you can, because he is one of only two electronics specialists available to you. His death can seriously hamper future missions.

Filatov, Genedy

Personal Information
Identification Number: RCT0069-A1772
Nationality: Russian
Specialty: Assault
Date of Birth: 12 February 1964
Height: 183 cm
Weight: 84 kg
Hair: Brown
Eyes: Brown
Gender: Male

Background
Born in Pskov, Pskovskaya Oblast in the former Soviet Union. No information on family. Served in army of former Soviet Union, 1981-85, including one tour in Afghanistan. Recruited by *Alfa* counterterrorist group, 1987. Operated in all major territories of the former Soviet Union and eastern Europe. Resigned from *Alfa* in 1991 in response to that organization's ambiguous response to the failed Soviet coup. Director of operations for private security firm, 1991-96. Returned to *Alfa* during its 1997 restructuring under the Russian Federal Security Service. Married, no children.

Filatov is a solid counterterrorism operative. His training and background are unorthodox by western standards, but he has a wealth of real-world experience from his years in the security forces of the former Soviet Union and numerous contacts across eastern Europe and Asia. His steady nerves and methodical approach to threats make him particularly valuable in combat situations. Do not let his world-weary manner mislead you; he is no pessimist, but, rather, a realist, and he prides himself on being the voice of reason and conservatism in any debate.

Attributes
Aggression: 82
Leadership: 82
Self-control: 87
Stamina: 83
Teamwork: 88
Demolitions: 62
Electronics: 36
Firearms: 91
Grenades: 85
Stealth: 70

Notes
Filatov is an average operative with good values in all attributes except electronics. Although he is not a leader, he does well in a support role.

Haider, Karl

Personal Information

Identification Number: RCT0007-A3709
Nationality: Austrian
Specialty: Assault
Date of Birth: 10 September 1975
Height: 196 cm
Weight: 117 kg
Hair: Brown
Eyes: Brown
Gender: Male

Attributes

Aggression: 100
Leadership: 75
Self-control: 71
Stamina: 96
Teamwork: 93
Demolitions: 42
Electronics: 55
Firearms: 89
Grenades: 71
Stealth: 74

Background

Born in Graz, Austria. Father is a petroleum distributor, mother a homemaker. Two siblings, a brother and a sister, both still in school. Joined the regular Austrian army in 1992. Transferred to *Gendarmerieeinsatzkommando Cobra* (GEK Cobra) in 1996. Trained with Germany's GSG-9 and Israel's *Sayeret Mat'Kal.* Participated in GEK Cobra raid on Deissenmayr GmbH headquarters in Vienna in 1998, single-handedly saving the lives of seven hostages. Married, 1999. No children.

In combat situations, Karl is unstoppable. He is extremely aggressive and will not hesitate to use any methods necessary to complete his mission. He is fanatical about protecting hostages and innocent bystanders, to the point of jeopardizing his own life. Off the job, he is soft-spoken and private, but has an iron determination.

Notes

Haider is one tough soldier, but he needs a strong leader. He provides good support for Chavez's team.

Hanley, Timothy

Personal Information

Identification Number: RCT0005-A1299
Nationality: Australian
Specialty: Assault
Date of Birth: 14 April 1965
Height: 187 cm
Weight: 85 kg
Hair: Blond
Eyes: Hazel
Gender: Male

Background

Born in Margaret River, Australia. Father is a winery fore-man; mother is a homemaker. Two siblings, a brother and a sister. Attended Australian Defense Forces Academy in Canberra, 1983-87. Upon graduation, the Special Air Service Regiment (SASR) recruited him into its newly formed 1st squadron; he remained with this unit when it was reorga-nized into the Australian Tactical Assault Group (TAG) shortly thereafter. He has served his entire career with TAG, except one tour with the Australian Intelligence Corps (AustInt), 1993-96. Has led counterterrorist teams on three continents and cross-trained with both U.S. Delta Force and British Special Air Service. Unmarried.

      Hanley is a career CT officer. He is a veteran of dozens of assaults and approaches even the most dangerous missions with easygoing good humor. Off duty, he is an experienced backpacker and mountaineer who has taken part in amateur expeditions to many of the world's major peaks. He is in superb physical condition and has demonstrated an ability to endure even the most extreme physical hardship.

Attributes

Aggression: 93
Leadership: 86
Self-control: 84
Stamina: 100
Teamwork: 86
Demolitions: 75
Electronics: 65
Firearms: 91
Grenades: 84
Stealth: 85

Notes

Hanley is another good support operative with good values across the board. In a pinch, you can use him even for demolitions work.

Lofquist, Annika

Personal Information
Identification Number: RCT0030-A3224
Nationality: Swedish
Specialty: Electronics
Date of Birth: 02 November 1966
Height: 179 cm
Weight: 68 kg
Hair: Blond
Eyes: Hazel
Gender: Female

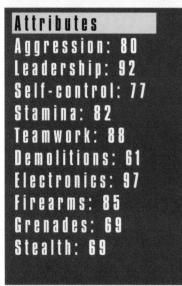

Attributes
Aggression: 80
Leadership: 92
Self-control: 77
Stamina: 82
Teamwork: 88
Demolitions: 61
Electronics: 97
Firearms: 85
Grenades: 69
Stealth: 69

Background
Born in Guteborg, Sweden. Father was a retired admiral in the Swedish Navy, now deceased. Mother is professor of Romance languages at Guteborg University and is active in *Miljupartiet de Gruna,* the Swedish Green Party. Three brothers. The entire family sails avidly. Attended Stockholm University, 1984-87; earned a B.S. in physics. After a stint as engineer with the Swedish semiconductor giant Microelektronik AB (1988-92), Lofquist joined the Stockholm police force as an expert on electronic surveillance. *Ordningspolisens Nationella Insatsstyrka* (ONI), the national rescue unit of the Stockholm police force, recruited her in 1994. From 1997 to 1999, she led ONI intelligence and surveillance teams in more than a dozen counterterrorist actions, including the high-profile 1998 Red Cell occupation of the trading floor of the Stockholm futures exchange. Unmarried.

Lofquist is an electronics genius. Her name is on 14 patents held by Microelektronik, her old employer, and she continues to consult with their engineers while serving as a member of the RAINBOW team. Most of her innovations are in the area of electronic eavesdropping. She is confident and courageous, but at times her lack of military training can lead her to overestimate her ability to handle a situation. Off duty, she keeps to herself, and lives alone on a sailboat in Saltsjobaden, outside Stockholm.

Notes
Lofquist is proficient in electronics and makes a good team leader. As with DuBarry, keep her safe. However, in a firefight, she is good with a gun.

Maldini, Antonio

Personal Information

Identification Number: RCT0023-A2009
Nationality: Italian
Specialty: Recon
Date of Birth: 14 October 1966
Height: 179 cm
Weight: 68 kg
Hair: Black
Eyes: Black
Gender: Male

Background

Born in Milano, Italy. Father manages a textile factory; mother is a homemaker. Five siblings. Attended *Universiti degli Studi di Ferrara,* 1984-88. Degree in chemistry. Joined l'Arma dei Caribinieri in 1989. On completion of training, he was assigned to the *Comando Carabinieri Antidroga,* the Caribinieri's antinarcotics agency. Transferred in 1995 to the *Gruppo Intervento Speciale* (GIS), Italy's elite counterterrorism team. Married since 1990. Three children.

Maldini's specialty is stealth. At GIS, his ability to occupy positions undetected by the enemy earned him the nickname "Invisible Man." He is in excellent physical condition and is quick on his feet. His demeanor is calm and somewhat aloof. Although a solid team member, he is too introspective to be a truly effective commander. Off duty, he is an amateur marathoner and has competed in races throughout Europe. Extremely intelligent and well-spoken.

Attributes

Aggression: 50
Leadership: 60
Self-control: 80
Stamina: 95
Teamwork: 80
Demolitions: 65
Electronics: 65
Firearms: 90
Grenades: 50
Stealth: 100

Notes

Maldini is extremely stealthy and can sneak up on enemies undetected. Use him for quiet strikes or to gain intelligence on enemy locations. He is no leader but is useful in either a support role or alone.

McAllen, Roger

Personal Information
Identification Number: RCT0011-A1932
Nationality: Canadian
Specialty: Demolitions
Date of Birth: 06 June 1964
Height: 185 cm
Weight: 95 kg
Hair: Brown
Eyes: Grey
Gender: Male

Attributes
Aggression: 70
Leadership: 70
Self-control: 70
Stamina: 98
Teamwork: 90
Demolitions: 97
Electronics: 71
Firearms: 96
Grenades: 100
Stealth: 70

Background
Born in Toronto, Ontario, Canada. Father is a senior officer with the Royal Bank of Canada. Mother deceased. He has one sister, who resides in Toronto. Joined Canadian Army as field engineer, 1981. One tour, 1981-85. Received advanced training in combat diving and explosive ordnance disposal. Upon discharge, joined the Royal Canadian Mounted Police (RCMP) and, in 1988, became a member of the Special Emergency Response Team (SERT), the RCMP's elite counterterrorism unit. When SERT was disbanded in 1993, he helped coordinate the transition of counterterrorist responsibilities to the Canadian Armed Forces' newly formed Joint Task Force Two (JTF-2). McAllen reenlisted in 1994 and became a full member of JTF-2 the same year. He has participated in counterterrorist actions on three continents, including JTF-2 extended operations against war criminals in Bosnia, 1996-97. Married, 1984; divorced, 1992. One child, a daughter, born 1986, lives with her mother in London, Ontario, Canada.

McAllen specializes in several areas. He is an excellent shot and is aggressive in combat situations, and so makes a good assault team member, but he also has extensive experience with bomb disposal and demolitions. He is an amateur power-lifter and his strength and stamina make him a formidable opponent. Team leads should be warned that he performs better as a subordinate than in a command position. He has a hearty, good-natured manner and spends his off-duty time socializing with a wide circle of friends, most military or ex-military men.

Notes
McAllen is proficient in demolitions and firearms and expert with grenades. Although he is not a leader, he is helpful as support when breaching doors and for additional firepower.

Morris, Gerald

Personal Information

Identification Number: RCT0047-A0781
Nationality: American
Specialty: Demolitions
Date of Birth: 24 December 1965
Height: 186 cm
Weight: 96 kg
Hair: Black
Eyes: Brown
Gender: Male

Background

Born in Birmingham, Alabama, USA. Father is a retired furniture salesman; mother is a homemaker. Two younger sisters, both still living in Birmingham. High school valedictorian; National Merit Scholar, 1982. Attended Rice University in Houston, Texas, 1983-87; earned a B.S. in material science and a B.A. in Russian literature. Joined the American Bureau of Alcohol, Tobacco, and Firearms (BATF) in 1988 as an agent in their explosives division. Earned an M.S. degree in inorganic chemistry from the University of New Orleans during leave of absence from BATF, 1992-94. His thesis, "Applications of Micro-stress Analysis in Accelerant Identification," is considered a landmark in the forensic analysis of bomb debris. Upon his return in 1995 to active duty in the BATF, he was assigned to their International Response Team (IRT). Since 1998, Morris has been on extended assignment in South Korea with the Korean counterterrorism task force, the National Police 868 Unit, training them in bomb detection, bomb disposal, and postbombing investigation techniques. His wife and two daughters currently live in Seoul, South Korea.

Attributes	
Aggression:	40
Leadership:	72
Self-control:	80
Stamina:	79
Teamwork:	89
Demolitions:	99
Electronics:	54
Firearms:	80
Grenades:	97
Stealth:	71

Morris is a team player who likes his operations run strictly by the book. His primary specialty is forensics, but he is also expert at setting and disarming of all types of explosive devices. Although he is experienced in conducting counterterrorist assaults from his years working with the 868 Unit, he prefers to take an indirect approach in hostage situations. Morris likes to spend his off-duty hours with his family. In his spare time he collects antique blues recordings and memorabilia.

Notes

Morris is very good with demolitions and grenades. Use him for support, much as you would McAllen.

Noronha, Alejandro

Personal Information

Identification Number: RCT0009-A1538
Nationality: Brazilian
Specialty: Assault
Date of Birth: 08 June 1959
Height: 175 cm
Weight: 70 kg
Hair: Brown
Eyes: Brown
Gender: Male

Attributes

Aggression: 91
Leadership: 91
Self-control: 91
Stamina: 82
Teamwork: 87
Demolitions: 50
Electronics: 32
Firearms: 94
Grenades: 75
Stealth: 73

Background

Born in Belo Horizonte, Brazil. His late father ran an import business. His mother is a homemaker. One older brother, two younger sisters. Attended college at the Brazilian military academy, *Colegio Militar do Rio de Janeiro* (CMRJ), 1977-81. Served two terms of duty with the regular Brazilian army before recruitment into the CounterTerrorist Detachment (CTD) of the 1st Special Forces Battalion in 1987. Since 1995 he has commanded one of CTD's three squadrons. He has cross-trained with the U.S. Delta Force, Chile's *Unidad Anti-Terroristes* (UAT), Agentina's *Brigada Especial Operativa Halcon,* and Columbia's Agrupacion *De Fuerzas Especiales Urbanas* (AFEU). In 1997, he was one of a group of senior Brazilian CTD operators who assisted the Peruvian armed forces in ending the occupation of the Japanese embassy by the Tupac Amaru Revolutionary Movement (MRTA). Married, 1985. His wife and two daughters live in Rio de Janeiro.

Noronha has spent most of his military career as a CT operator. He is well-known in the CT community, particularly in North and South America and has a reputation as a stern taskmaster. Although he has conducted actions in a variety of terrain and circumstances, he is particularly proficient in jungle operations and long-range intelligence-gathering. In combat situations, he is extremely aggressive and expects the same from any team that serves under him. He has no sense of humor and considers it unprofessional in others. His only passion (aside from work and family) is classical music and opera.

Notes

Noronha makes a good team leader. Although he is an assault specialist, you can assign his teams to other objectives, such as electronics or demolitions actions. He provides good leadership and protection to other types of specialists.

Rakuzanka, Kazimiera

Personal Information

Identification Number: RCT0027-A2057
Nationality: Polish
Specialty: Assault
Date of Birth: 29 February 1964
Height: 165 cm
Weight: 61 kg
Hair: Blond
Eyes: Brown
Gender: Female

Background

Born Kazimiera Koziol in Gdansk, Poland. Her father and brothers worked in the shipyards and she was active from an early age in the movement later known as *Solidarnosc.* In 1981, when she was 17, she was beaten seriously enough by police to require hospitalization; in 1982 she was arrested during a street demonstration and spent the following year in jail. Upon her release in 1983, she resumed activity in the Solidarity underground while working odd jobs in and around Gdansk. Married in 1986 to fellow activist Andrzej Rakuzanka. With the shifting of political winds in 1989 and the founding of the Republic of Poland, she was able once again to make public her affiliation with Solidarity. In 1990, she joined the reconstructed Gdansk police force and quickly moved into undercover work to battle the growing organized crime problem in the newly liberated country. In 1993, the *Grupa Reagowania Operacyjno Mobilnego* (GROM), Poland's newly formed counterterrorist unit. Initially involved purely in intelligence-gathering activities, in 1994, when her unit took part in Operation Restore Democracy, the American-led invasion of Haiti, she was promoted to full-fledged CT operator. She led her first assault team in 1998 and has since cross-trained with the U.S. Delta Force, Norway's *Beredskapstroppen,* and Finland's *Osasto Karhu.* Her husband and two daughters reside in Gdansk.

Rakuzanka is a survivor. Despite her unassuming appearance, she has an iron constitution and can endure extreme hardship. She is a strong team player and an excellent shot. She can be sarcastic but reserves her sharpest barbs for the rich and powerful. Friends and family call her "Kazi," colleagues "Kamikazi" (but never to her face).

Attributes

Aggression: 85
Leadership: 85
Self-control: 60
Stamina: 96
Teamwork: 94
Demolitions: 50
Electronics: 52
Firearms: 96
Grenades: 70
Stealth: 80

Notes

Rakuzanka is a good assault specialist in a support role. She is best at firearms, average in other areas.

Raymond, Renee

Personal Information

Identification Number: RCT0047-A1342
Nationality: American
Specialty: Assault
Date of Birth: 30 March 1968
Height: 172 cm
Weight: 64 kg
Hair: Brown
Eyes: Brown
Gender: Female

Attributes

Aggression: 75
Leadership: 79
Self-control: 90
Stamina: 91
Teamwork: 100
Demolitions: 30
Electronics: 23
Firearms: 97
Grenades: 85
Stealth: 96

Background

Born in Kansas City, Missouri, USA. Father is a retired U.S. Army colonel; mother is a homemaker. Two older brothers. Attended University of Oklahoma, 1986-89, under Reserve Officers Training Corps (ROTC) program, majoring in political science. Entered regular U.S. Army upon graduation. Served in Kuwait, 1991. Recruited into U.S. Special Operations Psychological Operations (PSYOPS), 1992. Served in Bosnia, 1996-97. In 1998, participated in U.S. Army trial introduction of women into special operations ground combat forces. Trained with 1st Special Forces Operational Detachment-Delta (1st SFOD-D, "Delta Force"). Married, 1993. Husband is a lieutenant in U.S. Army, stationed in Frankfurt, Germany. One child, a daughter, born 1995.

Raymond is self-reliant and resourceful. An excellent combat soldier, she is also well-versed in psychological warfare and understands how both soldiers and civilians react under the stress of combat. Although she is an experienced officer, she is too much of a loner to be at her best as team lead. Use her to maximum advantage in a support role. She talks little and weighs her words carefully when she does speak.

Notes

Raymond is not only excellent in combat, with great firearms and grenades attributes, but her great ability to move about quietly renders her useful for reconnaissance. Keep her in the support role; other team members are better leaders.

Sweeney, Kevin

Personal Information

Identification Number: RCT0049-A3964
Nationality: British
Specialty: Recon
Date of Birth: 30 March 1968
Height: 177 cm
Weight: 83 kg
Hair: Black
Eyes: Brown
Gender: Male

Background

Born in Birmingham, England. Father was a waiter, mother a cleaning woman. Two brothers, one younger, one older. Joined Birmingham Police Force as patrol officer, 1987. Promoted to detective, 1991. Spent the next five years working a variety of undercover operations in the Special Branch. In the fall of 1996, in collaboration with the British Security Service (MI5), coordinated a series of raids that broke the back of the "Field of Gold" terrorist underground in the British Isles. MI5 recruited him as an agent in 1997, and he left his position with the Birmingham force. Assigned to their counterterrorism branch (T Branch), and working out of London, Sweeney has planned and executed over two dozen covert actions in Great Britain and British territories. Unmarried.

Despite his youthful appearance, Sweeney is a master of covert operations. His knack for blending into the background served him well during his years working undercover on the streets of Birmingham. He is an excellent burglar and, despite his large build, can move quickly and quietly when he must. He is a good actor and maintains his composure in even the most stressful situations. Professionally, he is soft-spoken and earnest. He prefers consensus to confrontation.

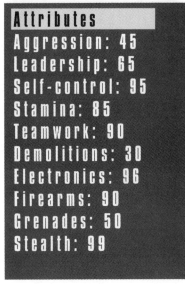

Attributes

Aggression: 45
Leadership: 65
Self-control: 95
Stamina: 85
Teamwork: 90
Demolitions: 30
Electronics: 96
Firearms: 90
Grenades: 50
Stealth: 99

Notes

Sweeney is not only stealthy and good with firearms, he also has a knack for electronics. He makes a good choice for sneaking into an area and disabling security systems and such. If he is not operating alone, use him in the support role.

Walther, Jorg

Personal Information
Identification Number: RCT0017-A1615
Nationality: German
Specialty: Assault
Date of Birth: 17 May 1974
Height: 190 cm
Weight: 105 kg
Hair: Brown
Eyes: Blue
Gender: Male

Attributes
Aggression: 76
Leadership: 97
Self-control: 90
Stamina: 96
Teamwork: 98
Demolitions: 71
Electronics: 89
Firearms: 96
Grenades: 83
Stealth: 97

Background

Born in Saarbrucken, Germany. Father is a safety engineer with Lufthansa German Airlines; mother is a homemaker. Three younger siblings—two sisters and a brother. Amateur archer, competing in Germany junior national championships, 1990. Entered the German Federal Border Police Force (*Bundesgrenzschutz*) in 1994, at the top of his cadet class. Stationed at Saarbrucken, 1994-98. Recruited into Germany's elite counterterrorist force, *-Grenzschutzgruppe 9-* (GSG-9) in 1998. Completed GSG-9 training in record time, again at the top of his class. Temporarily attached to GSG-9/1, the group's primary CT strike unit, before reassignment to RAINBOW. Married, 1996. No children.

Walther is the youngest member of the current RAINBOW team. His extraordinary drive and determination compensate for his inexperience in the field. He learns quickly and makes an exceptional team member who follows every order without hesitation or question. Although trained primarily in assault, he is well-versed in wiretapping and electronic surveillance. Bundesgrenzschutz command clearly is grooming him for advancement; his assignment to RAINBOW reflects the German government's long-term commitment to international CT collaboration.

Notes

Walther makes a great team leader. Not only is he good with firearms, but he is useful for electronics work, as well.

Woo, Tracy

Personal Information

Identification Number: RCT0047-A2715
Nationality: American
Specialty: Recon
Date of Birth: 14 July 1971
Height: 155 cm
Weight: 44 kg
Hair: Black
Eyes: Brown
Gender: Female

Background

Born in Los Angeles, California, USA. Father is a doctor, mother a lawyer. No siblings. Amateur gymnast, competing in West Coast regional championships 1987-88. Attended UCLA University 1989-92,; graduated with a B.A. in psychology. Joined Los Angeles Police Department in 1992; transferred to Metro Division Special Weapons and Tactics (SWAT) team in 1994, specializing in surveillance and negotiation. Commended for bravery for her role in ending the New Millennium occupation of Los Angeles City Hall in 1999. Unmarried.

Woo is expert in reconnaissance and surveillance. She moves quickly and quietly through terrorist-controlled areas and is skilled in the installation and removal of a variety of electronic intelligence-gathering devices. She handles command well but has an independent nature and has been known to argue with superiors. Her combat skills are average. Outspoken and self-reliant.

Attributes

Aggression: 50
Leadership: 75
Self-control: 85
Stamina: 96
Teamwork: 96
Demolitions: 30
Electronics: 85
Firearms: 80
Grenades: 50
Stealth: 98

Notes

Woo is a good support operative in recon missions. Although she is very stealthy, her combat and other skills are below average, (except for electronics, in which she is fairly proficient).

Yacoby, Ayana

Personal Information

Identification Number: RCT0022-A4242
Nationality: Israeli
Specialty: Recon
Date of Birth: 03 March 1973
Height: 163 cm
Weight: 57 kg
Hair: Brown
Eyes: Brown
Gender: Female

Attributes

Aggression: 95
Leadership: 65
Self-control: 70
Stamina: 95
Teamwork: 75
Demolitions: 30
Electronics: 86
Firearms: 97
Grenades: 60
Stealth: 97

Background

Born in Tel Aviv, Israel. Father is a greengrocer; mother died when she was three. One younger brother, professional soccer player, *Beitar Jerusalem.* Joined regular Israeli army, 1992. Transferred to *Sayeret Mat'kal* in 1995, where she served in the general staff reconnaissance unit. Mossad recruited her in 1997. Specializes in infiltration and intelligence gathering. In addition to her native Hebrew, speaks fluent English and Arabic. Unmarried.

Yacoby is master of the silent kill. Her training enables her to move stealthily into hostile territory and neutralize any threats. She is extremely intelligent with little tolerance for fools. The quintessential professional, she has complained about the "cowboy mentality" of some other team members. Ruthless in combat, in nonmilitary situations she may err on the side of excessive force.

Notes

As with most recon specialists, Yacoby is no leader. However, she is expert when it comes to firearms and stealth. Her lower self-control value means you should use her in support of good leaders.

CHAPTER THREE
TOOLS OF THE TRADE

The Rainbow team must use a number of items to complete its missions. Firearms first come to mind, but making an antiterrorist operative's job (and rescued hostages) safer requires other equipment. The diverse circumstances confronting team members involve using a variety of uniforms, as well. The following sections detail the many tools Rainbow uses to complete its missions.

FIREARMS

The firearms in the Rainbow arsenal are selected based on accuracy, firepower, and reliability. Each team member carries a primary weapon—a submachine gun, assault rifle, or shotgun—and a pistol. The needs of the mission determine which weapon is assigned. Sometimes stealth and silence are vital; other circumstances demand firepower at long range. Give your team members the best weapons for the tasks they must accomplish.

Heckler & Koch MP5A2

The preferred submachine gun of counterterrorist operatives around the world, Heckler & Koch's MP5 is renowned for its reliability and accuracy, even when firing on full-automatic. RAINBOW uses the 9mm MP5A2 fitted with single, triple, and full-auto trigger group.

Notes

This is the standard RAINBOW firearm, and it's one of the most accurate firearms available to your operatives. Unless you need long-range fire or stealth, this is the weapon to use.

Heckler & Koch MP5SD5

Terrorists throughout the world fear Heckler & Koch's MP5SD5. Its integral silencer is so effective that the bullet is quieter than the click of the bolt. RAINBOW uses the 9mm MP5SD5 whenever both accuracy and stealth are essential.

Notes

The MP5SD5 is essentially an MP5 with a silencer built on. Use this weapon when you must take out enemy units while maintaining stealth and secrecy. It's the only primary weapon with a silencer. Assign it to your recon teams.

Heckler & Koch MP5K-PDW

Heckler & Koch's 9mm MP5K-PDW is a compact version of the classic MP5. Its folding stock and light weight make it ideal for times when a full rifle or submachine gun is unmanageable and a handgun is a poor compromise. It comes equipped with the single and full-auto trigger group.

Notes

The PDW is RAINBOW's close-quarters submachine gun. Although not as accurate at the MP5A2, it's good for clearing rooms with full-automatic bursts.

CAR-15

A compact version of the M-16, the CAR-15 is commonly used when the firepower of an assault rifle is needed, but the weight and size is not. Commonly used by U.S. and Israeli special forces, it comes standard with a single, three round, and full-auto trigger group.

Notes

Issue the CAR-15 to firepower support teams. It's best used outside, but its compact size allows it to be used effectively inside buildings, as well. This weapon also has armor-piercing capabilities.

Colt M-16A2

When extra range or firepower is called for, RAINBOW turns to Colt's M-16A2. Tried and true, its 5.56 caliber easily pierces Level II body armor and it has the longest range of any standard RAINBOW weapon. The M-16A2 comes standard with a low-power holo-sight and single, three-round, and full-auto trigger group.

Notes

The M-16A2 is RAINBOW's heavy firepower. It's the standard infantry weapon of the U.S. military, but it's quite large by RAINBOW standards. This weapon is best for support-fire teams and is best used outside, where range is a factor. It's difficult to use in room-to-room combat because of its size. This weapon also has armor-piercing capabilities.

Benelli M1

Whether used for door breaching or highly lethal close-quarters combat, a good tactical shotgun is an essential part of all antiterrorist teams. RAINBOW uses the Benelli M1 tactical 12-gauge largely because its superb recoil characteristics enable a skilled operator to fire five rounds accurately in under a second.

Notes

The shotgun is best suited to breaching doors. It's useful against terrorists, as well, but if they have any body armor at all, a single blast rarely will take them down. Breaching teams should include at least one shotgun-armed member. Don't assign it to a team leader because he or she usually will be the first through a door and will need a high rate of fire with deadlier ammunition.

Heckler & Koch MK23

The extreme ruggedness, reliability, and match-grade accuracy of Heckler & Koch's .45 caliber Mark 23 ACP make it the handgun of choice for U.S. Special Forces.

Notes

Your team members will use their pistols rarely, usually if a primary weapon jams or runs out of ammo. Pistols are inaccurate at medium or long range. If you must use one, fire several times at your target: they allow only for single shots and it may take more than one to drop a terrorist, especially one in body armor.

The Mark 23 is one of the best pistols available to RAINBOW operatives. The weapon is accurate and the .45 round has the necessary stopping power.

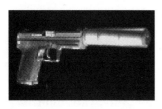

Heckler & Koch M23-SD

The specially designed sound and flash suppressor on this HKMK23 virtually eliminates muzzle flash and provides more than 35dB of sound reduction. It's an essential part of any RAINBOW mission that demands both firepower and discretion.

Notes

The Mark 23-SD is nearly as accurate as the standard MK23, and its silencer allows your team to kill without alerting others to your presence.

Heckler & Koch USP

Heckler & Koch's .40 caliber USP is favored by those desiring a balance of size and firepower.

Notes

This pistol is similar to the MK23, but it fires small-caliber ammunition, and so is a little lighter. It's usually a better idea to take an MK23 because of its greater punch.

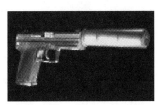

Heckler & Koch USP-SD

The Knight Armament silencer provides excellent sound suppression to the HK .40 USP.

Notes

Again, if you need a silenced pistol, the MK23-SD is a better choice.

Beretta 92FS

The Beretta Model 92FS is RAINBOW's 9mm pistol of choice. Its primary advantage is low recoil and a large magazine compared to the bulkier .45.

Notes

The Beretta fires a smaller caliber round than the Mark 23, so its magazine can hold more ammunition. If you're going to use a pistol a lot during a mission, then, this is a good choice. This is the standard sidearm of the U.S. military.

Beretta 92FS 9mm-SD

The specially designed sound and flash suppressor on this Beretta Model 92FS minimizes weight and length to maintain accuracy while boasting an impressive 32dB of sound reduction. It's the favored pistol among RAINBOW's recon specialists.

Notes

This is a great pistol for recon teams or any team that needs a silenced sidearm to supplement a nonsilenced submachine gun or assault rifle. Some missions may demand stealth at first and tremendous firepower later on. Use this pistol for the early kills.

EQUIPMENT

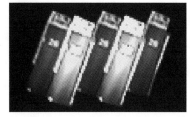

Flashbang

Flashbangs, with their bright flash and loud report, commonly are tossed into rooms prior to entry to "prepare" them. The seconds gained while potential hostiles recover from the stun effects can mean the difference between life and death to a tactical team. These also are known as distraction devices or stun grenades.

Notes

At least one member of each team should carry flashbangs. In fact, it's preferable for all to carry some, because clearing a large building may require a number of these devices. As a rule, use a flashbang if there's a chance an enemy occupies any room you're about to enter. The amount of stun time is determined by the attention state of the terrorist(s).

Fragmentation Grenade

The M61 fragmentation grenade is the standard-issue offensive grenade infantry uses throughout the world. Although its blast radius is small, an overhand throw is still necessary to safely clear the blast radius in the open.

Notes

These can clear a small room with a single blast. Take care when you use them during hostage rescues, unless you're certain the targeted room contains no hostages.

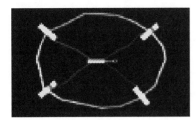

Breaching Charge

Breaching charges are used to remove doors explosively for rapid entry. You need not use a flashbang in conjunction with a breaching charge because they stun, wound, or even kill any nearby occupants.

Notes

These are great for entering a room quickly. Use them when breaching a door to a room containing both hostages and terrorists. Often terrorists will move to kill hostages as soon as a door is opened. The breaching charge will stun them, giving your team valuable seconds to enter and take down the hostiles.

Heartbeat Sensor

The heartbeat sensor can detect a human heartbeat even through thick layers of concrete.

Notes

The heartbeat sensor is very valuable. If the character you control carries one, select it as his or her active item. Then, when you hold down the mouse button, the sensor will scan at a longer range down a narrow arc, instead of the standard short range in all directions. Terrorists show up on the minimap as red dots and hostages as white dots. Use this sensor to see if a room is occupied before you enter it and help determine the type of force or restraint to use.

Demolitions Kit

This kit speeds both the placing and disarming of explosives. It contains basic electrical diagnostic equipment and mechanical tools essential to performing the job. Extra primer, detcord, and a variety of adhesives complete the kit.

Notes

Take this along only if explosives will be placed or disarmed. Assign it to a demolitions specialist.

Electronics Kit

This kit speeds up bug placement, security camera rewiring, and related electrical tasks. It includes a precise multimeter, miniature power supplies, breadboard, and digital analyzer. A full complement of jumpers, clips, and miscellaneous electrical parts round out the kit.

Notes

This is vital for getting through security systems. Assign it to electronics specialists.

Lockpick Kit

This kit speeds the picking of locks. Its primary component is a highly sophisticated auto-pick that can open most mechanical locks in a few seconds. For electrical keycard or swipe locks, the kit includes a classified system with presets for all major keycard variations.

Notes

Your team will need lockpick kits to get through some doors, especially without making a lot of noise, as with a shotgun breach or breaching charge.

UNIFORMS

RAINBOW operatives have access to a number of different uniform patterns, each designed for a certain environment (for example, urban, desert, woods). The patterns help make the team as inconspicuous as possible so they can take down the enemy before they're seen.

Each pattern is available in three weights. Light uniforms are basically for recon or other teams uninvolved in firefights. They're quieter and allow the wearer to move about stealthily. Heavy uniforms (a.k.a. "breaching" uniforms) incorporate the most body armor. However, they're bulky and make some noise, limiting wearer mobility and stealth. Breaching and demolitions teams should wear these. The medium weight uniform is the standard. It's appropriate for assault and other teams that need a balance between protection and ease of movement. As the commander, you must outfit your team members appropriately for the tasks they must perform.

Black/Light

This black lightweight uniform is perfect for nighttime missions and recon specialists. It consists of a lightweight Level IIa tactical vest capable of stopping low-powered pistol rounds. Standard soft-soled rubber boots, Nomex balaclava, and Nomex/Kevlar gloves round out the outfit.

Black/Medium

This black uniform is made of a Level II waist-length tactical vest and a Kevlar helmet, soft-soled rubber boots, Nomex balaclava, and Nomex/Kevlar gloves. It's RAINBOW's standard nighttime assault gear. The vest can stop most pistol fire and some submachine-gun fire.

Black/Heavy

This bulky black uniform consists of Level III body armor extending to the groin and can stop all but the most high-powered rifle rounds. It's preferred by demolitions experts, as the Kevlar helmet's faceplate offers excellent protection from flying debris. This version is especially suited for nighttime operations.

Camouflage/Light

This uniform is well-suited to jungle operations requiring great stealth. This jungle camo uniform consists of a lightweight Level IIa tactical vest (which will stop some low-powered pistol fire); lightweight, form-fitting jungle boots; Nomex balaclava, and Nomex/Kevlar gloves.

Camouflage/Medium

The Level II waist-length tactical vest that comes with this uniform can stop pistol rounds up to .40 caliber, as well as 9mm small-arms fire. This is RAINBOW's standard jungle gear, and also includes jungle boots, Nomex balaclava, and Nomex/Kevlar gloves. It's most useful for Central and South American and African operations.

Camouflage/Heavy

This bulky jungle camo uniform incorporates Level III body armor, camo boots, and Nomex/Kevlar gloves. It's slightly hotter and heavier than the other jungle camo uniforms, but affords more protection and can stop most small-arms fire, except that from higher powered rifles.

Desert/Light

This uniform is appropriate for desert operations where stealth is the primary factor. This uniform consists of a lightweight Level IIa tactical vest, lightweight desert boots, Nomex balaclava, and Nomex/Kevlar gloves. The vest will stop some pistol rounds.

Desert/Medium

This is the RAINBOW operatives' basic desert uniform. It includes a Level II waist-length tactical vest (which will stop most 9mm and smaller caliber weapons fire), as well as desert boots, Nomex balaclava, and Nomex/Kevlar gloves.

Desert/Heavy

This heavy desert camo uniform comprises Level III body armor, desert boots, and Nomex/Kevlar gloves. It affords far more protection than the other desert camo uniforms and can stop most small-arms fire, except that from higher powered rifles.

Street/Light

This urban camo uniform consists of a lightweight Level IIa tactical vest, soft-soled rubber boots, Nomex balaclava, and Nomex/Kevlar gloves. It's used mainly by recon specialists. Although it offers greater stealth, it protects against only low-powered pistol fire.

Street/Medium

Consisting primarily of a Level II waist-length tactical vest and a Kevlar helmet capable of stopping high-power pistol rounds, this is RAINBOW's alternative urban assault gear. Soft-soled rubber boots, Nomex bala-clava, and Nomex/Kevlar gloves round it out.

Street/Heavy

This heavy street camo uni-form incorporates Level III body armor extending to the groin. It's preferred by demo-litions experts, as the face-plate on its Kevlar helmet offers excellent protection from flying debris. This uni-form is very useful on urban assignments, and protects against most small-arms fire, except that from high-pow-ered rifles.

Tan/Light

This tan lightweight uniform is perfect for hot desert missions. It comprises a lightweight Level IIa green tactical vest that can stop low-powered pistol rounds and includes the standard desert boots, Nomex balaclava, and Nomex/Kevlar gloves.

Tan/Medium

This tan uniform includes a green Level II waist-length tactical vest, Kevlar Helmet, desert boots, Nomex balaclava, and Nomex/Kevlar gloves. This is RAINBOW's alternative desert assault gear. The vest can stop most pistol fire and some submachine-gun fire.

Tan/Heavy

This bulky tan uniform comprises Level III body armor extending to the groin and can stop all but the most high-powered rifle rounds. It's preferred by demolitions experts, as the faceplate on the Kevlar helmet offers excellent protection from flying debris. This version is especially suited for desert operations.

Urban/Light

Perfect for recon specialists, this uniform consists of a lightweight, Level IIa tactical vest that can stop low-powered pistol rounds. Standard soft-soled rubber boots, Nomex balaclava, and Nomex/Kevlar gloves round it out.

Urban/Medium

Primarily a Level II waist-length tactical vest and Kevlar Helmet capable of stopping high-power pistol rounds, this is RAINBOW's standard urban assault gear. It includes soft-soled rubber boots, Nomex balaclava, and Nomex/Kevlar gloves.

Urban/Heavy

This bulky uniform consists of Level III body armor extending to the groin and can stop all but the highest powered rifle rounds. Preferred by demolitions experts, the faceplate on the Kevlar helmet offers excellent protection from flying debris.

Woods/Light

Useful for operations in forests and rural areas where stealth is recommended, this woodland camo uniform comprises a lightweight Level IIa tactical vest, boots, Nomex balaclava, and Nomex/Kevlar gloves. Santiago Arnavisca especially favors woodland uniforms.

Woods/Medium

This woodland camo uniform includes a Level II waist-length tactical vest that can stop pistol rounds of up to .40 caliber and 9mm small arms fire. Boots, Nomex balaclava, and Nomex/Kevlar gloves round it out. It's most useful for European and North American operations.

Woods/Heavy

This bulky woodland camo uniform is made of Level III body armor, camo boots, and Nomex/Kevlar gloves. A little hotter and heavier than the other woodland camo uniforms, it affords far more protection and can stop most small-arms fire, except that from high-powered rifles.

Biosuit

This specially designed combat biosuit combines a Level IIa tactical vest with a full-body Level IV biohazard containment suit. Although its joints are specially reinforced, operatives wearing this suit in combat must use extreme caution to avoid compromising suit integrity.

It's time to practice the operations skills you must have to complete your real-world missions. The following tactics include breaching doors; room entry and clearing; hostage rescues; and other actions later missions may call for, such as defusing bombs and planting surveillance devices.

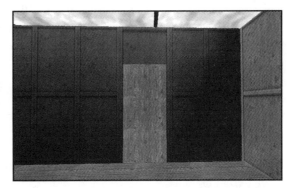

Fig. 4-1. Behind the closed door lies uncertainty. Breaching a door and entering a room is one of the most dangerous actions you'll perform.

BREACHING AND CLEARING

Most missions require your teams to enter buildings to rescue hostages, defuse bombs, or kill terrorists ("tangos"). Entering a room is one of the most dangerous things you'll do during a mission. You may not know what lies on the other side of the door, but those inside the room behind it will be waiting with weapons ready.

Tip

Before entering a room, use a heartbeat sensor to see what lies on the other side of the door.

Tip

Take care when using fragmentation grenades. They can kill hostages as well as your own people. As a rule, avoid using them during hostage missions.

Unless you're absolutely sure a room is clear, then, always enter with caution. The heartbeat sensor is a great device for determining whether a room is occupied; it can even distinguish between hostages and tangos. If your team isn't carrying one, always assume a room contains tangos. During hostage rescues, assume a hostage is inside, as well.

Your team is at a disadvantage as it enters a room. You need an edge: as soon as you breach a door, throw in a flashbang to stun the occupants. (Take care not to stun yourself in the process.) The stun grenade gives you a few precious seconds to enter the room and take down enemies before they can react. A breaching charge also works, blowing the door off and stunning the room's occupants at the same time. You can carry three flashbangs in place of one breaching charge, however; save the flashbangs for rooms with hostages.

You also can throw fragmentation grenades to "prepare" a room for entry. Be very careful, however, because they can kill team members and hostages as well as tangos. Avoid using them in hostage missions unless reconnaissance or a heartbeat sensor tells you a room is hostage-free.

Fig. 4-2. Throw a flashbang into the room to stun the tango before entering.

After you enter a room, you must clear it of enemies. If your team receives a "clear" order, it will spread out and do so automatically. Be wary of the room's other doors; more tangos may enter through them to investigate the gunshots.

The Kill Houses give you an opportunity to practice breaching and clearing.

Fig. 4-3. A tango is out in the open. Shoot quick before
he turns and fires at you!

Single-Room Kill House

The Single-Room Kill House lets you practice entering
and clearing a single room containing a single tango.
You can choose from three exercises. The first features
your character alone, the second adds a second operative, and the third gives you a team of four.

You may enter either door, but the one on the right
is usually the best choice. The tango may be anywhere
in the room, but he most often appears in the alcove to the
immediate right of the right-hand door or in between the two
doors. Have your MP5A2 at the ready as you open the door. If
the tango is directly in front of you, shoot before he does. You
may glimpse him if he's in the alcove. Throw a frag grenade in
to take him out or a flashbang to stun him so you can run in
and shoot.

In the third exercise, when you approach the door
on the right, one of your team members will tell you
to back up. He'll open the door and throw in a flashbang. Once it goes off, rush into the room before the
tango can recover.

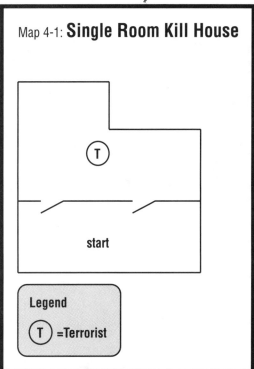

Map 4-1: **Single Room Kill House**

T

start

Legend

(T) =Terrorist

Fig. 4-4. In the third exercise, another team
member will open the door and throw in a flashbang. If the tango hides to the right of the door,
however, it may not stun him.

Double-Room Kill House

The second Kill House contains two rooms with a tango in each, a more difficult scenario. There are three exercises for this Kill House, as well. The first uses you alone; the second gives you command of a team of four operatives. The third exercise has two teams of three operatives each. You control Blue Team.

In the first exercise, it's easier to enter the left door first. The tango usually is in the back corner and you can drop him before he has a chance to react. Advance into the room and approach the other doorway carefully. The second tango is in the other room. If you can't see him through the doorway, he may be behind the wall to your right. Throw in either a frag grenade to kill him or a flashbang to stun him so you can rush in and use your submachine gun.

Fig. 4-5. There's no tango in sight as you open the door. That means he waits in ambush to the left or right.

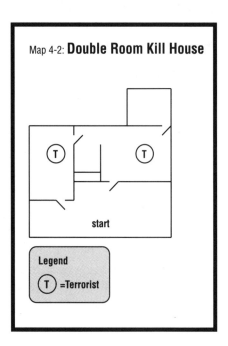

Map 4-2: **Double Room Kill House**

start

Legend

(T) =Terrorist

The second exercise uses the same strategy as the first. Try going through the door on the right this time.

The final exercise puts you in command of Blue Team. Red Team awaits Go code Alpha. Press Q to get them moving. They'll enter the left door while your team goes through the right. Take care not to shoot the other team once you're in the first room.

Fig. 4-6. You command two teams for the third exercise. Give Go code Alpha to order Red Team through the left door while Blue Team goes through the right.

RESCUING HOSTAGES

Missions where you must rescue hostages require extra caution. Often hostages are held in rooms guarded by at least one tango. Although the recon information you get prior to a mission may give locations for the hostages, they may have been moved. The heartbeat sensor is the best way to identify a room's occupants before you rush in.

Fig. 4-7. Hostages will stay put unless your Rule of Engagement mode is set to Escort. Then they'll follow you around like puppies–hopefully to safety.

Don't use frag grenades when entering a room that contains hostages. You'll kill not only the tangos, but the hostages, as well. Instead, throw in either a flashbang to stun everyone or, better, use a breaching charge. The charge will blow the door open and stun the room's occupants at the same time.

After breaching a door, exercise caution as you enter. Avoid firing your weapons at full-automatic; the spread could hit a hostage. Instead, use the three-round burst (or the single shot if the three-round isn't a choice). Things move fast in *Rainbow Six*, and it's easy to develop an itchy trigger finger. Learn to use caution and to pick your targets with care.

Office Kill House

This is a very difficult Kill House to clear. You begin in the outside hall. Two doors provide entry to the office area, which contains six small rooms. What makes this particularly deadly is the way all the offices are lined up across from each other with open doorways. As you enter one office, a tango across the hall can shoot you in the back.

Note

When throwing a flashbang into a room with a hostage, there is a risk that the guard will execute the hostage if they see the grenade. If possible, try to throw a flashbang out of the guard's line of sight. You can see which direction the guard or guards are facing by using a heartbeat sensor and zooming in on the map.

Tip

Whenever you open a door to a room containing a hostage and a tango, the tango usually moves to kill the hostage, so you must act quickly. You can't just stand in the doorway looking around, or you'll be too late.

The first of the three exercises gives you a single team of four operatives; the second, two teams of four operatives; the third, one team of two and two teams of three. The Kill House contains four tangos and one or two hostages. Two tangos wait in interior hallways and the other two in offices.

When you're on your own, enter the right-hand door. There should be a tango right in front of you or just around the corner. Take him down, and then look around the corner. Shoot the second tango at the far end of the long hall. If he's not there, go back into the outside hall: he's sneaking up behind you. Only two tangos to go.

Start at one end and check the two rooms, throwing in a flashbang before entering each. If you hear a groan when the stun grenade goes off, you know there's someone inside. After clearing both rooms at one end, do the same at the other end. You should have found at least one of the terrorists and a hostage or two. Leave the hostages for now. The final tango waits in one of the two center rooms; or, if two tangos remain, there's one in each center room. In this case, you should enter the top room from the right and the bottom from the left to limit your exposure to fire from the other tango.

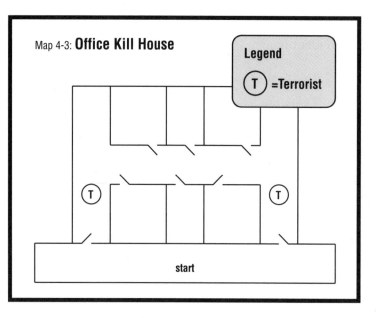

Map 4-3: **Office Kill House**

Legend

(T) =Terrorist

start

Tip

Use flashbangs not only to stun tangos, but to determine which rooms they're hiding in. If you hear a groan when the flashbang goes off, there's someone inside. Either rush in immediately or throw another flashbang in first.

Fig. 4-8. The facing, open doorways create a deathtrap unless you're smart and use caution. Remember to use flashbangs to stun waiting tangos before entering the rooms.

In the second exercise, you command Blue Team, on the right. Red Team on the left awaits Go code Alpha. Press Q to give them the go, and they'll enter the left door and advance into the offices to search for the hostages. You must lead Blue Team through the right door and do the same. The third exercise puts you in control of Blue Team, with two operatives, near the right door. Red Team, with three, is next to you, and Green Team is at the left door. Code Alpha orders Red and Green teams to enter their respective doors, taking out the two hall tangos in the process. Bravo (W) orders them to search the offices for the hostages. Blue Team's job is to escort the hostages to safety. Delta (R) orders the two other teams to return to their starting positions.

Your other teams probably will take casualties. If you watch them, you can see why. They don't use their flashbangs before entering the rooms, so any tangos present can fire before the operatives even know they're there.

Two-Story Kill House

If you can get through the "graduation" Kill House without losses, you're ready to go operational. The Kill House is a two-story building with an accessible roof. There are six tangos inside and one hostage on the second floor.

In the first exercise, you have a single team of four. The second gives you two teams of four: as one team enters the front door, the other goes up the outside stairs to the roof. The third exercise has three teams: two go in the front door while the third enters from the roof.

Fig. 4-9. The third exercise has three teams. Red and Green clear the rooms, while Blue waits to escort the hostages to safety.

You begin near the front door of the building. Open it. A tango stands directly in front of you. Take him out and wait for a second tango to appear. Once he's down, run in and turn right. A tango descends the stairs to investigate the noise. Drop him and run to the stairs at the other end of the building. If your clip is low, reload as you run.

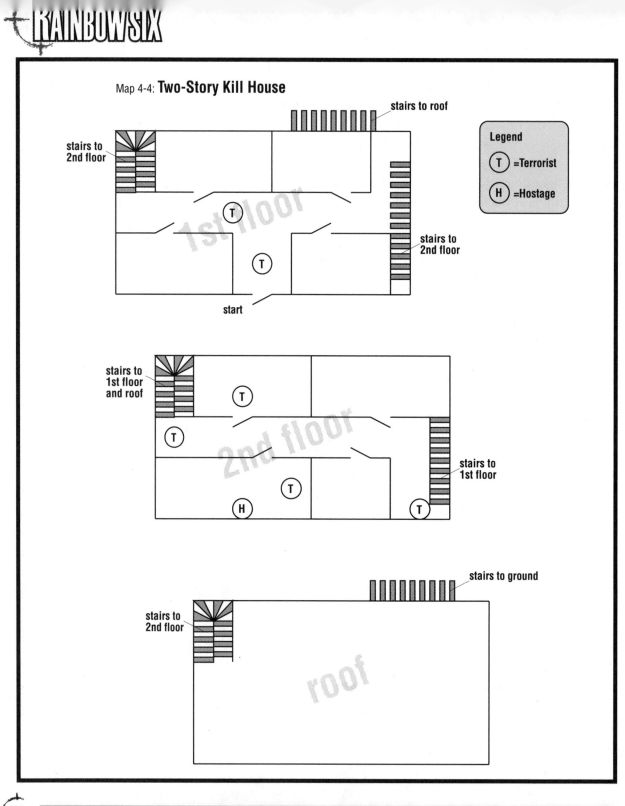

Map 4-4: **Two-Story Kill House**

stairs to roof

stairs to
2nd floor

Legend

T =Terrorist

H =Hostage

1st floor

T

T

stairs to
2nd floor

start

stairs to
1st floor
and roof

2nd floor

T

T

T

H

stairs to
1st floor

T

stairs to ground

stairs to
2nd floor

roof

At the stairs, sidestep up so you face the landing at the second floor. Take out the tango at the top and reload again. Sidestep up the last few steps until you're in the hallway and can barely see the tango in the room to the right. There's also one to the left. Both have a view and a shot at the hostage in the room on the right, so you must act carefully, but quickly. Throw a flashbang at the tango on the right and follow up with your submachine gun while he's still partially concealed by the doorframe. Then quickly run into the left room to kill the final tango before he gets the hostage.

Fig. 4-10. Right as you open the door, a tango is waiting to die.

OTHER TYPES OF ACTIONS

Your missions may call on you or your other teams to perform special actions, anything from disarming a bomb or deactivating a security system to downloading computer files or tapping a phone. These may sound difficult, but you need only walk to the object and press keypad 0 to perform them.

To have a team not under your control or a specialist on your team who's not the leader perform the action, place a waypoint next to the object in the planning phase and assign an action to the waypoint. Then, when you approach it, the specialist will walk to the object and do what needs to be done.

Fig. 4-11. Sidestep up the stairs to surprise the tango at the top.

Fig. 4-12. You must act quickly to take out the last two tangos. Shoot the one on the right after throwing a flashbang and while he's still half-hidden by the doorframe.

The adage "If you fail to plan, you plan to fail" applies to this game more than to any other. The planning stage is the most important, and that's where you'll spend the most time during operations. Most missions take only a few minutes to execute but can take an hour or more to plan and fine-tune. The planning stage is broken down into seven screens. Each contains important information or requires you to do something to prepare for the mission. In the following sections, we'll look at each screen, and then go over mission-planning basics.

BRIEFING

This is the first screen in the planning stage, where you receive valuable information regarding your current mission. Your objective—what you must accomplish to complete the mission—lies in the center of the screen. In Recruit campaigns, you need achieve only the primary objective. The Veteran level requires a secondary objective and the Elite a third. The higher the level of gameplay, the more terrorists you'll face and the harder they'll be to kill.

On the left side of the screen are quick briefings by Control (your commander), and other useful information. Your mission orders display below the briefings. Study them carefully to learn what you must do and what you're up against.

Fig. 5-1. The Briefing Screen

INTEL

Although the Intel screen isn't vital for achieving
your particular mission, it provides background
and story line for the campaign. It displays your
past mission success and shows how it affects the
campaign. The four categories of information this
screen displays are people, organizations, newswire,
and miscellaneous.

Fig 5-2. The Intel Screen

Fig 5-3. The Roster Selection Screen

ROSTER SELECTION

You choose operatives for the current mission from
the Roster Selection screen. It displays background
information on each member of RAINBOW,
including his or her abilities and health status.
When you select your operatives, you needn't pick
them in order or by team. You can organize them
later.

KIT

You arm your team from the Kit screen. For each operative, you can select a primary and secondary weapon, additional items to carry (these fit into slots one and two), and a uniform. Although you can assign everyone the same things, you'll probably need to customize individual kits for specific jobs.

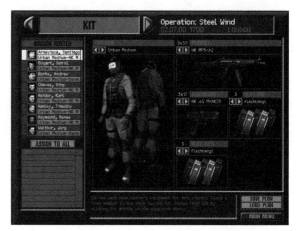

Fig 5-4. The Kit Screen

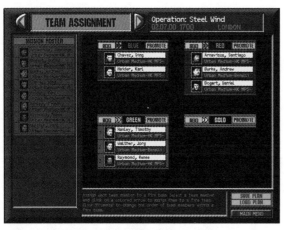

Fig 5-5. The Team Assignment Screen

TEAM ASSIGNMENT

You'll organize your operatives into teams from this screen. You can take only eight people with you, divided into a maximum of four teams. Teams can comprise no more than four operatives each. You can create two teams of four or four teams of two or anything in between.

PLAN

You'll spend the most time at the Plan screen. It provides a recon report of probable locations of hostages, terrorists, and landmarks. You'll plot waypoints for each of your teams here and give them special orders or commands. Once the action starts, you control only your team. At each waypoint you can change Rules of Engagement regarding speed and mode–how fast the team moves to the next waypoint and how they respond to others on the way. You can give breaching instructions at waypoints, as well.

Fit. 5-6. The Plan Screen

You can acquire some control over other teams using Go codes. There are four in all. When a team reaches a waypoint with a Go code, it will wait for you to issue that code before advancing. This way you can synchronize your teams' activities. For example, if all teams get the same Go code near a building's entry point, they'll wait for the code to enter at the same time. The section "Planning a Mission" covers the Plan screen in greater detail.

EXECUTE

From the Execute screen you'll choose a team to control, and then start the mission.

PLANNING A MISSION

Mission-planning can be difficult and time-con-suming. If you fail a mission or are unhappy with the results, you may return to the planning stage and try it again. Rarely will you execute a perfect mission your first time through. How-ever, the better your plan, the better the execution.

Fig 5-7. The Execute Screen

You'll take the following steps when you plan a mission, not necessarily in this order.

Briefing

First, read through all the briefings to learn what the situation is and determine the nature of your job. You'll find the latter in the mission orders and objective. Listen to Control and to John Clark. They may offer some insights. Next, go to the Intel screen to get background information on the mission.

Recon

At the next screen, pick a team member at random. (You must select one to advance to the next screen.) Continue past the Kit screen, assign the operative to a team, and then move on to the Plan screen. It doesn't matter which team you place your operatives in. You'll reassign them later.

At the Plan screen, go to the box in the lower left and select Recon to learn the actual or proba-ble locations of hostages and terrorists in the mission area. The Landmarks category will provide important information about terrain and structures—whether a trellis is climbable or an entrance barricaded, for example. Learn as much as you can about what you face. Then decide how many teams you'll need to accomplish the mission and what their tasks will be.

Set Waypoints

Change the Recon box to Waypoints, select a team, and begin plotting waypoints. The first must be within a starting location and the last within an ending location. Determine the team's entry into a building, their route to that spot, how they'll reach their objective, and, finally, how they'll get out. Use Go codes to coordinate team activity. For example, it's usually a good idea to have all teams enter a building at the same time. But in some cases, one team may have to complete a task before another team can continue.

In addition to Go codes, you can give teams breaching instructions at each waypoint near a doorway. For example, you can order them to use a flashbang or frag grenade, or even a breaching charge. Such orders are important, because computer-controlled teams won't do these things unless they're instructed to. Set these for your own team, as well. If you want a demolitions specialist on your team to breach a door a certain way, order it at that waypoint or you'll have to do it yourself using the equipment you're carrying.

Rules of Engagement tell your teams how to behave as they advance to the next waypoint. There are two types of ROEs—speed and mode.

Speed tells the team how fast to move and how careful to be when targeting and firing weapons. "Blitz" instructs the team to move as quickly as possible and to fire at just about anything that moves. Use Blitz only when there are no friendlies in the area. "Standard" speed is a basic walk; the team exercises a bit more caution before firing. Teams assigned "Safety" speed will move slowly and take deliberate aim at well-identified targets before firing, perhaps even risking their own safety. When approaching areas where hostages are located, change the speed to "Safety."

Mode tells a team how to act and react. Teams with "Clear" orders will clear the enemies from the area around the waypoint—usually the middle of a room or at a breach point. "Engage" orders a team to move along their path while attack-

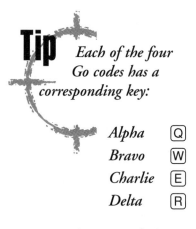

Tip *Each of the four Go codes has a corresponding key:*

Alpha   Q
Bravo   W
Charlie   E
Delta   R

You may use each Go code more than once. For example, you may want to assign all Alpha codes to Blue Team, Beta Codes to Green, and so forth.

ing targets of opportunity. "Advance" makes movement the team's main concern. Team members will attack only enemies blocking their path. Heartbeat sensors are used only on teams with Advance orders. After the team rescues a hostage, it must escort the hostage to safety. If a team approaches a hostage in any other mode, the hostage will stay put. Escort mode tells the hostage to follow the team. When escorting a hostage, the team should follow a secure route cleared of tangos to the end point.

After planning waypoints for all teams, consider making a few short notes on what each Go code does for quick reference later.

Building Teams

You know how many teams you'll have and the tasks for each. Now it's time to choose operatives from the Roster Selection screen.

Delete the members you chose earlier and start from scratch. First, choose an operative with good leadership ability for each team. Teams that must breach their way in need a demolitions specialist. Next, assign specialists, such as electronics, if the mission calls for them. Finally, fill in the teams with assault specialists. Place those with poor self-control or teamwork values with stronger leaders. With the operatives and their assignments fresh in your mind, go to the Team Assignment screen and place them into teams, with the leader at the top of each list.

Pass the Ammo

Distribute firearms and equipment to your assembled teams. RAINBOW is well-funded, so you have as many of each weapon or item as you need. Equip your teams appropriately for their tasks. For example, if they must breach a door with a charge, at least one member of the team must carry a breaching charge. The same goes for flashbangs and frag grenades.

Finally, suit your operatives in appropriate uniforms. Choose inconspicuous patterns and weights appropriate for the task. Breachers should wear heavy uniforms; recon teams will don light ones to stay quiet. Most team members should wear medium-weight uniforms that provide a balance of protection and mobility.

Start the Mission

Your teams are ready, so go to the Execute screen next. You've invested a lot of time into planning this mission, so it's a good idea to save it here. This way, if you must start over, you can make small adjustments to your plan instead of going back to the beginning. Finally, select the team you'll lead, and then begin the mission.

Good luck!

Mission Failure?

If you fail a mission or get a lot of your people killed in a successful mission, go back to planning and try again. Study who got killed and where to determine the planning changes you need to make. For example, if a team was massacred entering a room, order them to throw a frag grenade before going through the doorway. You may also need to change a team's ROE for a certain waypoint. Think of each failure as a learning experience.

Tip

Consider replaying the mission if even one team member dies, especially in the early missions. Losing one member per mission will leave you short of trained, experienced professionals for the last few.

CHAPTER SIX
THE MISSIONS

The *Rainbow Six* campaign comprises 16 missions. You must complete each to advance to the next. This chapter provides all the information you'll need to get through the missions.

The strategies are for the Veteran (medium) difficulty level, requiring you to complete both the primary and secondary objectives before advancing to the next mission. Recruit level requires you to complete only the primary objective. Elite missions usually are more difficult because they have more terrorists to kill.

The mission strategies include orders and objectives, who to take, what they should carry, how to organize them, and, finally, how your teams can go about accomplishing the mission, with instructions for each. Use these instructions during the planning phase to set waypoints and issue special instructions and Go codes.

These strategies aren't set in stone. You may find something to add or change to fit the plans to your playing style. Experiment. The best plan is the one that succeeds.

The walkthroughs for each of the missions are organized to facilitate planning. Included is a list of the teams and the way they should be organized. Next, in the strategy section, you are given a brief summary of what must be done to complete the mission, followed by in-depth strategies for each of the teams. While it may seem these team strategies are for you to play out, they are organized by team for simplicity during the planning phase. Just because Blue Team's strategy is first does not mean their actions precede those of other teams. Instead, plot Blue Team's waypoints following their team strategy and continue for each of the other teams. The Additional

Fig. 6-1. The ambassador hides on the second floor. Act quickly: the terrorists will kill him if they find him.

Notes section then ties all the strategies together and lets you know when to issue Go codes. This last section should be used during the actual mission rather than the team strategies that should have already been given to the teams during the planning phase. In many missions, one team must complete a task before another team can continue. Go codes allow you to hold a team at a point in the mission until the task has been completed. The code then releases them to continue. Some missions have only a few Go codes while others have several. They can also be used to hold a team before a difficult area so you can take control and lead them through yourself.

MISSION 1–OPERATION: STEEL WIND

02.07.00 1700 London

Mission Orders

Members of Free Europe, a British neo-Nazi group, have seized the Belgian embassy. The ambassador is hiding in an office on the second floor and has so far avoided capture. Other embassy workers may be trapped inside, as well. Surveillance indicates terrorists on all three floors of the complex.

Objectives

1. Rescue the ambassador.
2. Rescue the staff member.

Mission Data

Difficulty Level	Terrorists	Hostages	Other
Recruit	9	1	None
Veteran	9	2	None
Elite	17	2	None

Team Assignments

Blue Team

Operative	Primar	Secondary	Slot 1	Slot 2	Uniform
Chavez	MP5-A2	.45 Mark 23	Frag Grenade	Flashbang	Urban Medium
Yacoby	MP5-A2	.45 Mark 23	Door Charge	Flashbang	Urban Medium

Red Team

Operative	Primary	Secondary	Slot 1	Slot 2	Uniform
Walther	MP5-A2	.45 Mark 23	Frag Grenade	Flashbang	Urban Medium
Raymond	MP5-A2	.45 Mark 23	Door Charge	Flashbang	Urban Medium

Green Team

Operative	Primary	Secondary	Slot 1	Slot 2	Uniform
Bogart	MP5-A2	.45 Mark 23	Frag Grenade	Flashbang	Urban Medium
Arnavisca	MP5-A2	.45 Mark 23	Door Charge	Flashbang	Urban Medium

Gold Team

Operative	Primary	Secondary	Slot 1	Slot 2	Uniform
Hanley	MP5-A2	.45 Mark 23	Frag Grenade	Flashbang	Urban Medium
Burke	MP5-A2	.45 Mark 23	Door Charge	Flashbang	Urban Medium

Map 6-1: **Operation:Steel Wind, Mission 1**

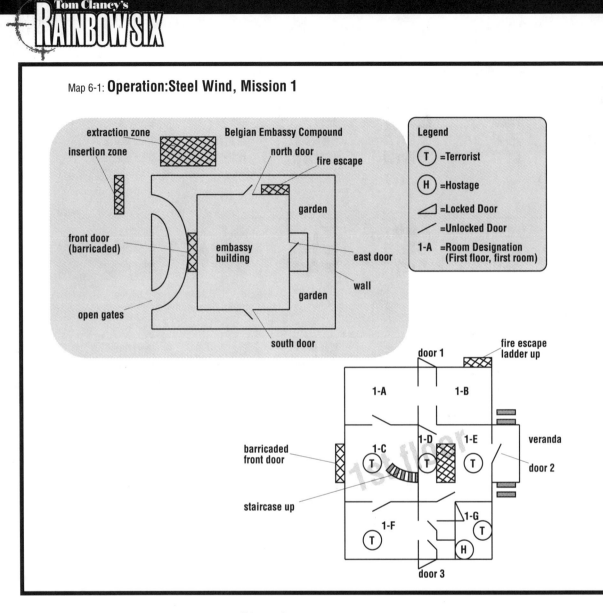

Strategy

Your mission is to enter the Belgian embassy and rescue the hostages. Although it would be safer for your team to take their time on this mission, you must get to the ambassador on the second floor as quickly as possible.

At the beginning of the mission, the tangos have not yet found him. If they do, they'll kill him. Therefore, you must get to him as quickly as possible, protect him from the tangos and then get him out to safety. An embassy staffer is being held

Map 6-1, cont.: **Operation:Steel Wind, Mission 1**

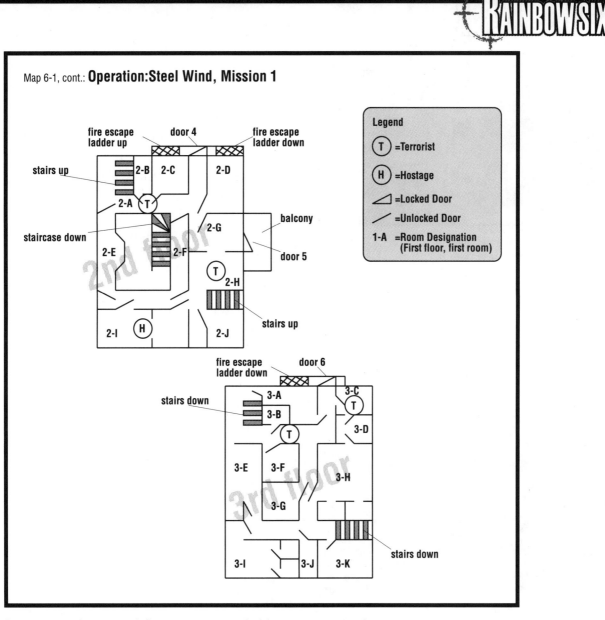

hostage on the ground floor room, guarded by a tango. Get her out, as well.

The front door to the embassy is barricaded and all outside entrances locked. Two of your teams have orders to rescue the hostages and escort them out; the other two teams will clear the first and second floors of the embassy and clear a way out for the escort teams. Both insertion and extraction zones are outside the walls of the embassy compound.

Fig. 6-2. Blue Team must climb up the side of the veranda to reach the second-floor balcony and enter the embassy building.

Blue Team

Take control of Blue Team, whose task is to rescue the ambassador. This team's entry point is through the balcony overlooking the garden. Climb up the veranda to reach the balcony door. Place a breaching charge on the door. Now wait for Alpha.

When the other teams finish placing their charges, give the code and blow the door. Enter 2-G and advance to 2-H. There's a terrorist in one of these rooms; you may encounter another near the stairs on your way to 2-I, where the ambassador is hiding. Wait until Green Team makes it to the hallway outside this room and awaits a Go code. Give the Bravo code and follow Green down the main staircase to foyer 1-C, through room 1-A, and then out door 1 to safety outside the compound walls.

When you're outside of the embassy building, you can switch to another team, such as Gold.

Red Team

Red Team's task is to clear the first floor of the embassy. After receiving Go code Alpha, they enter door 1 with a breaching charge. Take out the tango in the hall or area 1-D before checking rooms 1-B and 1-A. Go through 1-D to enter foyer 1-C and take down the tango there. Next, kill the tango in 1-F and open door 3. Return to the foyer to cover the staircase until you receive code Delta. Then move out door three, leading the way to safety for Gold Team.

Fig. 6-3. Red Team waits for Go code Alpha to blast the door open and begin clearing the first floor.

Green Team

Green Team's task is to clear the second floor and lead Blue Team out of the building. Climb up the fire escape along the north side of the building and enter at door 4 with a breaching charge at code Alpha. Advance down the hall carefully. Throw a frag at the tango in hall 2-A and check the other rooms along this hall. Be careful of tangos coming down the stairs by 2-B. Advance to the elevated walkway at 2-E and on toward 2-I.

Hold at the southern door to 2-E and wait for code Bravo. Then lead Blue Team and the ambassador to the staircase through 2-F, down to the foyer, 1-C, and out door 1 to safety.

Gold Team

Gold Team enters through the back door, 2, at the veranda with a breaching charge at code Alpha. Enter room 1-E, then advance to the door to 1-G. Hold for code Charlie. Issue this code after Red Team completes its clearing and awaits Delta. At Charlie, open the door and take out the terrorist guarding the staff member. Move quickly or the tango will kill the hostage. There's no time for a flashbang, just enter and fire, careful not to hit the hostage. Hold here until you receive code Delta; then exit the building, escorting the hostage out door 3 with Red Team.

Notes

This mission requires a lot of coordination. All teams enter the embassy at code Alpha. Code Bravo tells Blue and Green to exit. Code Charlie orders Gold to enter the room with the staff member and the tango. Code Delta orders Gold and Red teams to leave the building. It's a good idea to control Blue Team first, at least until they're on their way down the stairs. Then switch to Gold Team, which is holding for Charlie. You can probably do a better job taking out the tango in 1-G. He's usually in the corner diagonally right across from the door. Give the code before going in to avoid confusing the waypoints as you enter. When both hostages make it to the extraction zone, the mission ends.

Fig. 6-4. Once it receives code Bravo, Green Team leads Blue out of the building.

Fig. 6-5. Gold Team must rescue the staff member. The terrorist guarding her will kill her shortly after you open the door to the room. You must shoot first.

Fig. 6-6. Everyone made it out safely. It may take a few tries to get this outcome, especially without wounding any operatives.

MISSION 2-OPERATION: COLD THUNDER

04.15.00   0200
Congo

Mission Orders

Hutu rebels have seized a World Health Organization research station run by the Horizon Corporation. They're holding the research staff hostage. A leading expert on filoviruses, Dr. Catherine Winston, is among the captives.

The rebels hold the hostages in an abandoned colonial villa. A large rebel camp lies nearby, but observers report few enemy troops in the building. You will be inserted by helicopter in a small clearing a short distance from the villa.

Fig. 6-7. Dr. Winston is held under guard on the second floor of the house.

Objectives
1. Rescue Dr. Winston.
2. Rescue WHO doctor.

Mission Data

Difficulty Level	Terrorists	Hostages	Other
Recruit	10	1	None
Veteran	13	2	None
Elite	18	2	None

Team Assignments

Blue Team

Operative	Primary	Secondary	Slot 1	Slot 2	Uniform
Chavez	MP5-SD5	9mm 92FS-SD	Primary Mag	Empty	Camo Light

Red Team

Operative	Primary	Secondary	Slot 1	Slot 2	Uniform
Yacoby	MP5-SD5	9mm 92FS-SD	Primary Mag	Empty	Camo Light

Green Team

Operative	Primary	Secondary	Slot 1	Slot 2	Uniform
Maldini	MP5-SD5	9mm 92FS-SD	Primary Mag	Empty	Camo Light

Strategy

This is a fairly easy, straightforward mission. You can complete it with only two teams or even a single operative. This strategy uses three teams to give you practice using Go codes.

Your teams begin in the jungle, a short distance from the outpost. A path leads to the outpost. Tangos stand guard outside the main house, and inside, as well. Dr. Winston is on the second floor and the other doctor is in the basement. Both are under guard.

This is a night mission, so stealth is your best tactic. Bring only silenced weapons. You'll need no flashbangs or frag grenades for this mission.

Blue Team

Chavez is Blue Team. Walk down the jungle path toward the barn. Before you get there, walk a bit toward the tents to the north. Press CTRL to bring up Sniper view. Use this magnified view to take out the tango near the fire.

Look toward the house. You should see one or two other guards. Take them out at long range. The three-round burst works well for this. Three guards cover the rear of the house.

Note

If you can't select a suggested RAIN-BOW operative due to death or wounds, choose a comparable replacement.

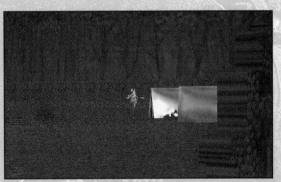

Fig. 6-8. Use Sniper view to take out tangos at long range. The tangos won't know what hit them, and, because you use silenced weapons, other tangos won't know what happened.

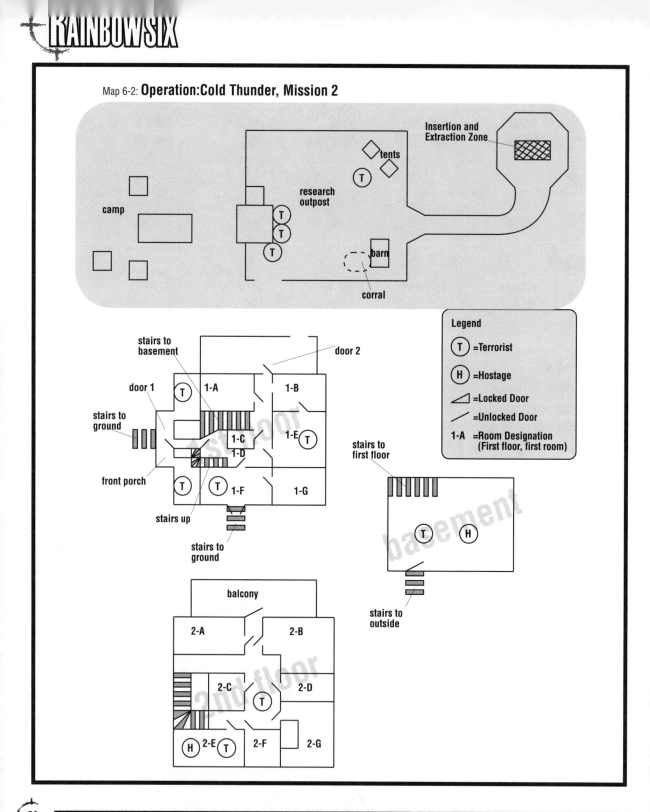

Map 6-2: **Operation:Cold Thunder, Mission 2**

Insertion and
Extraction Zone

tents

research
outpost

camp

barn

corral

Legend

(T) =Terrorist

(H) =Hostage

◿ =Locked Door

╱ =Unlocked Door

1-A =Room Designation
(First floor, first room)

stairs to
basement

door 2

door 1

1-A

1-B

stairs to
ground

1-C

1-E

1-D

front porch

1-F

1-G

stairs up

stairs to
ground

stairs to
first floor

1st floor

basement

stairs to
outside

balcony

2-A

2-B

2-C

2-D

2nd floor

2-E

2-F

2-G

Walk around the barn to the other side before taking out the remaining guard. Now walk along the south wall to an opening. Advance outside the wall to the corner. As you round it, you'll see a guard on the front porch. Take him out, and then sidestep until you have a shot at the second porch guard.

With the outside clear, backtrack into the compound and walk to the basement entrance. Move carefully down the stairs and take out the tango guarding the doctor. Take care, or he'll kill the doctor.

Now wait for code Alpha. Give codes Bravo and Charlie. When Red Team arrives to pick up the hostage, code Alpha gives you the go to advance up the stairs into the house. Exit the basement stairway carefully. Green Team will be clearing the first floor. When he holds for Charlie, head up the staircase to the second floor. One tango moves about the second floor, so use caution to locate and take him out. You can usually find him in room 2-C or 2-D.

Dr. Winston is being held in room 2-E. Slowly advance to the doorway and kill the guard inside before he can kill the hostage. Quickly head back down the stairs to the basement. Give code Charlie to order Green Team to follow you out, covering your rear, and move quickly to the extraction zone.

Fig. 6-9. Take out the guards on the front porch before heading into the basement. One has a view to the basement entrance.

Fig. 6-10. Escort Dr. Winston down the stairs to the basement, and then out to the extraction zone.

Red Team

Red Team's job is simple: get the WHO doctor to safety. This team should advance to the barn and hold for code Bravo. Once the code is given, move along the south wall to the basement, walk to the hostage, and escort him to the extraction zone along the same path. Wait at the extraction zone for the other two teams.

Fig. 6-11. Red Team escorts the WHO doctor out of the basement to safety.

Green Team

Green Team must clear the first floor of the main house. Wait at the barn with Red Team until you get code Charlie. Then advance past the rear of the house and enter it through door 2. Check all the rooms, beginning with 1-A. There are tangos in 1-E and 1-F. Hold at the foot of the stairs until you get another Charlie code. Then follow Blue Team into the basement and out to the extraction zone.

Notes

Alpha codes are for Blue Team; Bravo and Charlie codes are for Red and Green, respectively. Try this mission solo, controlling a single operative with no supporting teams, and follow the Blue Team strategy: Leave the doctor in the basement, go upstairs and clear the first floor, and then the second, to rescue Dr. Winston. Head back to the basement, pick up the other doctor, and take both to the extraction zone.

MISSION 3-OPERATION: ANGEL WIRE

06.25.00   **0530**
North Sea

Mission Orders

Members of the Phoenix Group, a radical environmentalist organization, have taken over a North Sea oil drilling rig. The terrorists have planted explosive devices on the rig and threaten to blow it up if their demands aren't met.

You'll be inserted by inflatable boat at the base of the rig's legs. Two tiers of catwalks allow movement between the legs. Above, the two-level main structure contains machine rooms and the crew's quarters. Surveillance indicates a bomb on each level of the main structure. The detonator for both bombs lies in another room on the top level. If the terrorists detect your presence they'll use this trigger to set off the explosives.

After completing your mission, you'll be extracted by helicopter from the rig's upper deck.

Your team has two new operatives in this mission.

Fig. 6-12. Tangos hide in several places around the oil rig. They're dressed like workers, so don't be fooled. The two hostages are together in the same room, under guard.

Objectives

1. Prevent bomb detonations.
2. Rescue oil rig workers.

Mission Data

Difficulty Level	Terrorists	Hostages	Other
Recruit	10	0	2 Bombs
Veteran	14	2	2 Bombs
Elite	19	2	2 Bombs

Team Assignments

Blue Team

Operative	Primary	Secondary	Slot 1	Slot 2	Uniform
Chavez	MP5-SD5	.45 Mark-SD	Frag Grenades	Heartbeat Sensor	Black Medium
Arnavisca	MP5-SD5	.45 Mark-SD	Frag Grenades	Heartbeat Sensor	Black Medium
Morris	MP5-SD5	.45 Mark-SD	Demolition Kit	Empty	Black Heavy

Green Team

Operative	Primary	Secondary	Slot 1	Slot 2	Uniform
Walther	MP5-SD5	.45 Mark-SD	Frag Grenades	Flashbangs	Black Medium
Raymond	MP5-SD5	.45 Mark-SD	Flashbangs	Heartbeat Sensor	Black Medium

Gold Team

Operative	Primary	Secondary	Slot 1	Slot 2	Uniform
Bogart	MP5-SD5	.45 Mark-SD	Frag Grenades	Flashbangs	Black Medium
Burke	MP5-SD5	.45 Mark-SD	Frag Grenades	Heartbeat Sensor	Black Medium

Fig. 6-13. The rooms on the oil rigs are often filled with obstacles. A heartbeat sensor will tell you what you're up against before you enter a room.

Strategy

The strategy for this mission isn't difficult, but the execution can be tricky. Although you can only control one team at a time, hold your teams at Go codes immediately before a task, and then switch to that team to perform the task. After completion, switch to the next team and complete its task, and so forth.

Each of your three teams has a specific task in this mission. One must get to the detonator to prevent any tangos triggering the bombs. Another team must disarm the bombs as the third team rescues the hostages. Keep things as quiet as possible until the detonator is safe, so the tangos don't set off the bombs.

Blue Team

Blue Team's task is to disarm the bombs. They should begin in tower 3, the southwest leg of the oil rig. Climb the stairs to level 7 and wait for code Alpha. Then make your way to tower

Map 6-3: **Operation:Angel Wire, Mission 3**

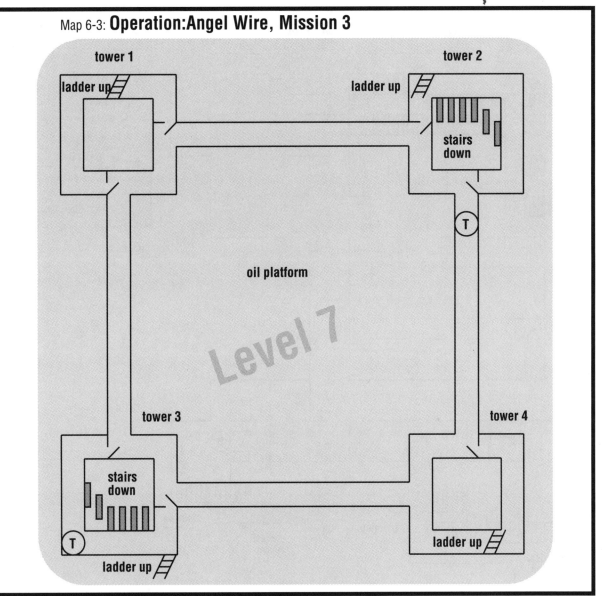

tower 1

ladder up

tower 2

ladder up

stairs
down

oil platform

Level 7

T

tower 3

tower 4

stairs
down

ladder up

T

ladder up

4, watching for a couple of tangos on the catwalks. Climb the ladder and quickly move across the catwalk to enter room 8-D. Inside, await another code Alpha. You'll receive it after both Green and Gold teams accomplish their tasks.

After you get the code, advance to hall 8-C, room 8-E, and then 8-F. Use the heartbeat sensors to locate tangos in 8-G. Take them both out and have Morris disarm the bomb. (You must put this action into the plan if you want Morris, a noncontrolled team member, to disarm the bomb.)

One bomb down and one more to go.

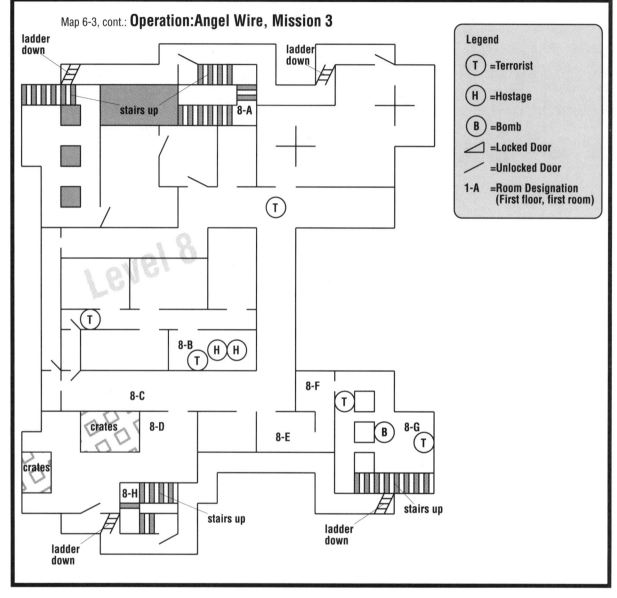

Map 6-3, cont.: **Operation:Angel Wire, Mission 3**

ladder
down

ladder
down

stairs up

8-A

Legend

(T) = Terrorist

(H) = Hostage

(B) = Bomb

◁ = Locked Door

╱ = Unlocked Door

1-A = Room Designation
(First floor, first room)

Level 8

(T)

(T)

8-B (H) (H)
(T)

8-C

8-F

(T)

crates

8-D

8-E

(B)

8-G

(T)

crates

8-H

stairs up

ladder
down

ladder
down

stairs up

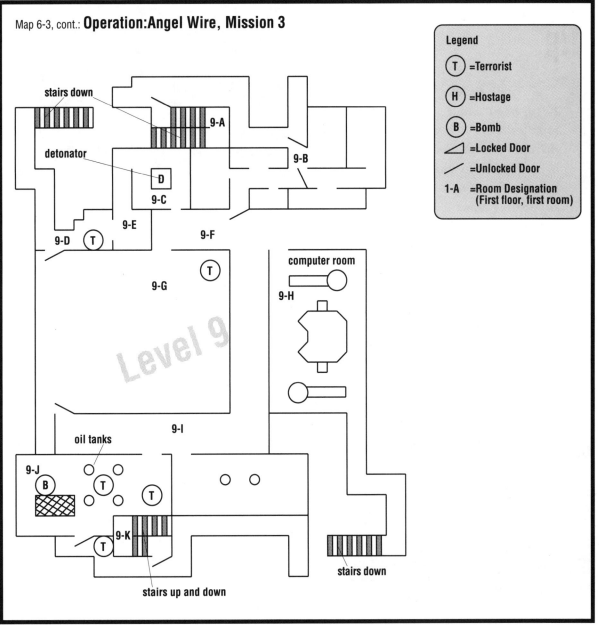

Map 6-3, cont.: **Operation:Angel Wire, Mission 3**

stairs down

9-A

9-B

detonator

D

9-C

9-E

9-D (T)

9-F

9-G (T)

computer room

9-H

Level 9

9-I

oil tanks

9-J

B

T

T

9-K

T

stairs down

stairs up and down

Legend

(T) =Terrorist

(H) =Hostage

(B) =Bomb

◁ =Locked Door

╱ =Unlocked Door

1-A =Room Designation
(First floor, first room)

Fig. 6-14. Morris disarms the first bomb. This doesn't take long: he's carrying the demolitions kit and is an expert in this field.

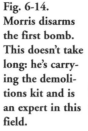

Tip

A team's Rules of Engagement mode must be set to Advance for the heartbeat monitor to work when assigned to a supporting team member. This tells the other team member to pull out the sensor and begin scanning.

Head up the stairs in the south part of the room and go through room 9-H to hall 9-I. There's a terrorist outside room 9-J and two more inside. Drop them all, using the sensor to locate them before rushing the room. Disarm the final bomb and wait for code Delta. When you get the code, head out the south door to stairway 9-K and climb it to the helipad–your extraction zone.

Green Team

Green is the hostage rescue team. It follows Blue Team to room 8-D, where it will await code Bravo. When you get this code, move out into hall 8-C and then through the door to 8-B.

There's a tango in this room with the two hostages; another tango moves around in the nearby rooms or hallway. When the room is clear, escort the hostages to stairway 8-H, up to level 10 and the extraction zone.

Gold Team

Gold Team must reach the detonator and prevent any tangos from setting off the bombs. Its insertion point is tower 2, in the northeast. Climb the stairs to level 7 and await code Alpha. When you get it, climb the ladder to level 8; then advance along the catwalk to stairway 8-A. Move up the stairs to level 9, and then out the door and along another catwalk to 9-B. Inside, wait for code Charlie.

Fig. 6-15. Green Team must take care when entering the room containing the hostages. They're dressed like their terrorist guard. Shoot the one with the gun and you'll be OK.

After Charlie, move out into hall 9-F, and then into computer room 9-H. A tango patrols the catwalk from the south end of the room. Wait until he approaches the doorway and drop him. This will make Blue Team's job a little safer.

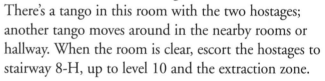

Now get to the detonator in room 9-C. No one should be in there, so go through 9-E to kill the tango in 9-D. Backtrack to 9-C, and then take out the tango in 9-G by tossing a frag grenade around the corner. Return to 9-C and guard the room until you get code Delta. Then advance as quickly as possible to stairway 9-K and up to the extraction zone on level 10.

Notes

All the Go codes may be a bit confusing, but you're using them as gates to halt team movements at critical points, where you'll take control. It doesn't matter which team you control first. Just get the team to the first code Alpha waypoint. When all teams await this code, give it to them. All will exit the tower stairwells and head to their next Go code location. There are two tangos on level 7. The Go code lets all your teams move at once into their first potential firefight. You should control Blue Team as it crosses the catwalk to tower 4. Scan the catwalks for tangos. If none are nearby, use sniper view and take them out at long range. Continue following waypoints until you reach the next Go code. Each team now awaits a different code. This is where each must perform its particular task. Choose Gold Team and give code Charlie. After they secure the detonator and reach code Delta, switch to Green Team.

Green Team awaits Bravo. Give the code and then rescue the hostages. After you kill the two tangos in the area near the hostages, switch to Blue Team. Green will automatically take them to safety at the extraction zone.

Your final task is to disarm the bombs. Give Blue Team the Alpha code and do your stuff. After taking care of the second bomb, you must hold for code Delta, the code that orders Blue and Gold teams to the extraction zone. Give it, and both teams will run for the helipad.

Fig. 6-16. Gold team guards the detonator until Blue Team can disarm the bombs.

Fig. 6-17. Everyone made it safely to the helipad.

MISSION 4-OPERATION: SUN DEVIL

08.03.00 0630
Brazil

Mission Orders

American and Brazilian workers have been kidnapped from the site of a new research station under construction in the Amazon rain forest. Ramon Calderon, a local drug lord, is responsible. Calderon runs his operation out of a former sugar cane plantation on the Brazil-Colombia border.

Intelligence reports Calderon's stronghold is well-guarded. Guards armed with automatic weapons patrol inside and outside the house. The workers are being held in the basement, and Calderon's bedroom lies on the second floor.

You'll be inserted on the road to Calderon's house, a short distance from his front gate. Return with the hostages to this location to be airlifted out.

Objectives

1. **Rescue workers.**
2. **Kill Ramon Calderon.**

Fig. 6-18. You'll really need the heartbeat sensors once you get your teams inside the plantation house. Tangos are hiding in corners, waiting to ambush you.

Mission Data

Difficulty Level	Terrorists	Hostages	Other
Recruit	12	2	None
Veteran	14	2	None
Elite	17	2	None

Team Assignments

Blue Team

Operative	Primary	Secondary	Slot 1	Slot 2	Uniform
Walther	MP5-A2	.45 Mark 23	Flashbang	Frag Grenade	Camo Heavy
Arnavisca	MP5-A2	.45 Mark 23	Heartbeat Sensor	Frag Grenade	Camo Heavy

Red Team

Operative	Primary	Secondary	Slot 1	Slot 2	Uniform
Chavez	MP5-A2	.45 Mark 23	Flashbang	Frag Grenade	Camo Heavy
Raymond	MP5-A2	.45 Mark 23	Heartbeat Sensor	Frag Grenade	Camo Heavy

Green Team

Operative	Primary	Secondary	Slot 1	Slot 2	Uniform
Bogart	M-16A2	.45 Mark 23	Primary Mag	Empty	Camo Heavy
Yacoby	M-16A2	.45 Mark 23	Primary Mag	Empty	Camo Heavy

Strategy

This mission is straightforward but difficult to execute. One of your teams will be the outside fire support and will clear the exterior of the house from a distance. The other teams will enter the building. As one rescues the hostages, the other will find the drug lord and execute him. As in the previous mission, you should control each team during its most difficult task to prevent unnecessary casualties. All the tangos have automatic weapons and are very dangerous. Heartbeat sensors allow infiltrating teams to detect tangos hiding in ambush around corners.

Fig. 6-19. You can take out half the tangos from long range while they're outside the plantation house.

Blue Team

Blue Team's job is to rescue the hostages. Advance to the wall around the plantation house and hold behind it until code Alpha. Then run to door 2 and hold for another Alpha code. So far, you should have avoided any tangos. Green Team already has

Fig. 6-20. Throw frag grenades around corners to take out tangos waiting in ambush.

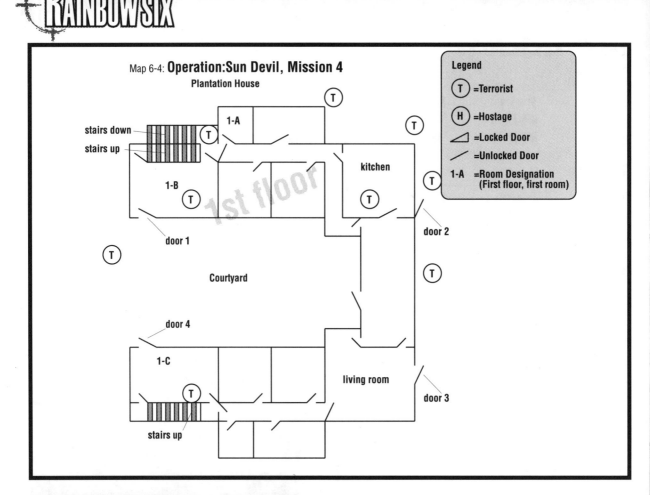

Map 6-4: **Operation:Sun Devil, Mission 4**

Plantation House

Legend

(T) =Terrorist

(H) =Hostage

◿ =Locked Door

╱ =Unlocked Door

1-A =Room Designation
(First floor, first room)

stairs down

stairs up

1-A

1-B

kitchen

door 1

door 2

Courtyard

door 4

1-C

living room

door 3

stairs up

1st floor

Fig. 6-21. You must kill the tango guarding the hostages quickly before he can kill them—or you!

taken down the outside guards, as well as the ones in this part of the house. Enter the kitchen, and then move on to the hallway. There may be a tango at the far end of the hall. If not, he's probably in room 1-A. Use the heartbeat sensor to locate both him and the tango in 1-B. Rather than expose your team to fire, throw frag grenades around the corners of these rooms to take them out. Next, head downstairs to the basement.

Hold at the basement door until you receive another Alpha code. Carefully open the door and take out the terrorist in your line of sight. If you can't see him, wait until he comes out into the open. Then move carefully into the basement. Another tango guards the two hostages in room B-A.

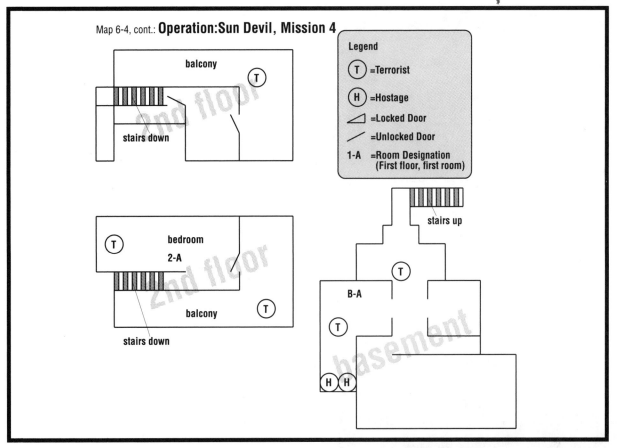

Map 6-4, cont.: **Operation:Sun Devil, Mission 4**

balcony

T

2nd floor

stairs down

bedroom

2-A

T

2nd floor

balcony

T

T

stairs down

Legend

(T) =Terrorist

(H) =Hostage

◿ =Locked Door

╱ =Unlocked Door

1-A =Room Designation
(First floor, first room)

stairs up

T

B-A

T

basement

(H)(H)

Advance along the right-hand wall and then side-step left to put the tango in your sights. Shoot quickly before he can fire at you or the hostages.

With the basement clear, escort the hostages to the kitchen and await code Delta. Then head to the extraction zone.

Red Team

Red Team's task is to execute the drug lord, Ramon Calderon. First, advance to the wall around the plantation house and hold for code Alpha. Then run to wait near door 3 for code Bravo. You should only face two tangos during this mission. The first is in room 1-C. Use the heartbeat sensor to find

Fig. 6-22. The drug lord has fallen, but it could be your team, if they aren't careful. Calderon packs some heavy firepower and waits for you to run around the corner. A frag grenade will take him out or at least stun him.

Fig. 6-23. Take out the tango on the balcony first with the M-16A2. Then wait for six more tangos to come to take a look. Kill them all, and the outside of the house is almost clear.

Fig. 6-24. Red Team awaits its Go code to enter the house and execute its task.

him, and then throw a frag grenade around the corner into the room to take him out. Then make your way up the stairs. Hold at the top for code Bravo again.

Calderon is in the room at the top of the stairs, around the corner. Use the heartbeat sensor to find his exact position, and then throw a frag grenade around the corner. Rush in after the grenade goes off. If it missed him, he'll be stunned and you can take him down before he recovers.

Go back down the stairs and hold in room 1-C for code Delta. Then make your way to the extraction zone.

Green Team

Green Team provides fire support and clears the outside of the plantation house of all tangos. Because all their shots will be from long range, members are assigned M-16A2s for more firepower.

Begin by moving to the wall around the plantation house. Using an edge for cover, take out the guard on the balcony using Sniper view. A second tango waits to the right of the house and a third to the left. Drop them both. Before moving farther, wait for code Charlie.

Four more tangos will come from the left to investigate the gunfire. Kill them all, and then proceed left toward the barn. Go around it and along the base of the cliff until you have a shot at the guard on the other balcony. After eliminating him, hold for code Delta. This gives you the go-ahead to return to the extraction zone.

Notes

Begin in control of Green Team, because its job is the first you must do. After all seven tangos are down on this side of the house, code Delta tells the team to head around to the other side to take out the tango on the opposite balcony. When all is clear, give code Alpha. Blue and Red teams will run to their positions outside the house at doors 2 and 3, respectively.

Switch to Blue Team and give code Alpha. Lead Blue Team to free the hostages. The tangos waiting in ambush make this difficult, and you probably can do better than the computer. The next Alpha code is at the door to the basement. When the hostages are free, lead them back to the kitchen to await Delta.

Switch to Red Team. Give code Bravo, and then advance to room 1-C. The next Bravo code is at the top of the stairs, in the drug lord's bedroom. After Calderon is dead, return downstairs. Finally, give code Delta to order all teams to return to the extraction zone.

MISSION 5-OPERATION: GHOST DANCE

08.27.00   1830
Barcelona

Mission Orders

Left-wing terrorists have taken over the Pirate Adventure ride at the WorldPark amusement park in Barcelona. They hold several tourists hostage in the center of the attraction.

Park security has sealed off the area around the ride. A main entrance and a back alley give access to the building. A system of maintenance passages and catwalks connects the attraction's public areas.

Your team receives two new operatives for this mission.

Objective

1. Rescue all hostages.

Fig. 6-25. This mission takes place in an amusement park's Pirate Adventure ride.

Fig. 6-26. Control room 2 looks out over the attraction's main entrance. However, your teams will use the back door.

Fig. 6-27. You must reach the hostages before their terrorist guards execute them.

Mission Data

Difficulty Level	Terrorists	Hostages	Other
Recruit	10	5	None
Veteran	12	5	None
Elite	14	5	None

Team Assignments

Blue Team

Operative	Primary	Secondary	Slot 1	Slot 2	Uniform
Chavez	MP5-SD5	.45 Mark-SD	Flashbangs	Frag Grenades	Urban Light
Yacoby	MP5-SD5	.45 Mark-SD	Flashbangs	Heartbeat Sensor	Urban Light

Red Team

Operative	Primary	Secondary	Slot 1	Slot 2	Uniform
Noronha	MP5-SD5	.45 Mark-SD	Flashbangs	Frag Grenades	Urban Light
Raymond	MP5-SD5	.45 Mark-SD	Flashbangs	Heartbeat Sensor	Urban Light

Green Team

Operative	Primary	Secondary	Slot 1	Slot 2	Uniform
Walther	MP5-SD5	.45 Mark-SD	Flashbangs	Frag Grenades	Urban Light
Burke	MP5-SD5	.45 Mark-SD	Flashbangs	Heartbeat Sensor	Urban Light

Gold Team

Operative	Primary	Secondary	Slot 1	Slot 2	Uniform
Bogart	MP5-SD5	.45 Mark-SD	Flashbangs	Frag Grenades	Urban Light
Arnavisca	MP5-SD5	.45 Mark-SD	Flashbangs	Heartbeat Sensor	Urban Light

Fig. 6-28. Blue Team clears the catwalks overlooking the ground floor.

Strategy

This is a tough mission. The terrorists guarding the hostages have instructions to kill them if anyone attempts a rescue. You must use the greatest caution and stealth to infiltrate the amusement attraction and converge on the area where the hostages are held.

There are catwalks and passageways above the ground floor. You must clear these of tangos prior to the rescue. Use four teams in this mission: two can clear the catwalks and control rooms, while the other two secure the ground floor, except for the hostage room. Then, when all teams are in position, all will take out the tangos near the hostages. Finally, escort the hostages to safety.

Blue Team

Blue Team must clear the catwalks suspended above the attraction. Enter door 1 at code Alpha; then climb stairway 3 and wait for another Alpha code. When it comes, rush into area 3-D. There's one tango there and another at ground level you can take out from above.

Next, advance to 3-F, drop the tango there, and then make your way toward 3-E. Hold at the passage to 3-C and wait for Delta. When this code to rush the hostage area comes, run out into 3-C, take out the tango on the catwalk, and then do what you can to help the teams below. Finally, make your way through 3-D to stairway 3 and out to the extraction zone.

Red Team

Red Team's job is to get the hostages to safety. They enter door 3 at code Alpha, and then wait outside the door to 1-C. When you get another Alpha, rush in, take out the tango guard there, hop into the water, and wade to the entrance to 1-A. Stay out of sight until you receive code Delta. Then rush into 1-A and take out the guards. Concentrate on the two tangos nearest the hostages; they have orders to kill them. Escort the hostages back through 1-C and out door 3 to the extraction point.

Green Team

Green Team must secure the midlevel passageways to the control rooms. Enter the building through door 2 at code Alpha.

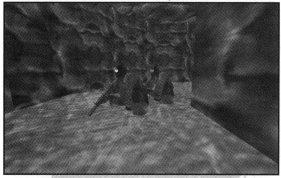

Fig. 6-29. Red Team makes its way through the tunnels toward the hostages.

Fig. 6-30. Green Team clears out control room 1, overlooking the area where tangos hold the hostages.

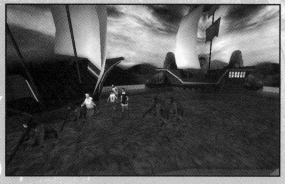

Fig. 6-31. Gold Team waits patiently for the other teams to get into position. When they get code Delta, they'll rush in to kill the tangos in the room with the hostages.

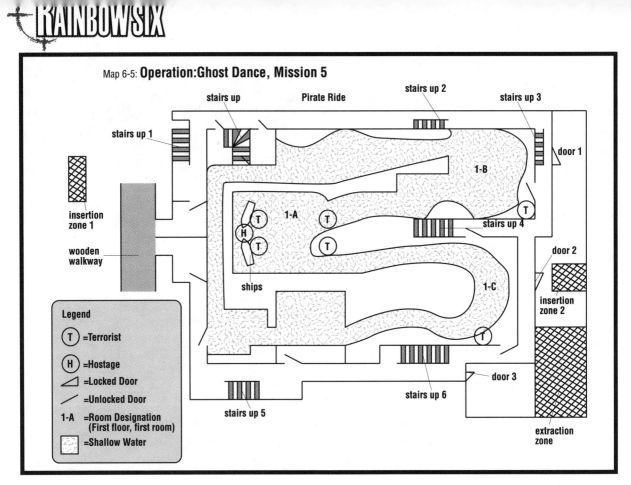

Map 6-5: **Operation:Ghost Dance, Mission 5**

Legend

(T) = Terrorist

(H) = Hostage

◁ = Locked Door

╱ = Unlocked Door

1-A = Room Designation (First floor, first room)

▨ = Shallow Water

Note

This is a very interesting level. Take some time to walk around and explore it. It's also great for multiplayer games.

Immediately head up stairway 4 and over to control room 2. Take out the tango there, and then run back to control room 1. Wait outside the door until you get code Delta; then enter the control room and clear it. The tango there may leave before you get the Delta code, so just take him out. Then you can make your way back to the extraction zone.

Gold Team

Gold Team provides support for Red Team. Enter door 1 at code Alpha. Then move over near the door to room 1-B. At the next code Alpha, enter the room and take out the tango inside (if Blue Team hasn't already). Then move over near the pirate ship and wait for code Delta. This tells you to rush into room 1-A and take out the terrorists before they can kill the hostages. Follow Red Team out through 1-C and cover their rear all the way to the extraction zone.

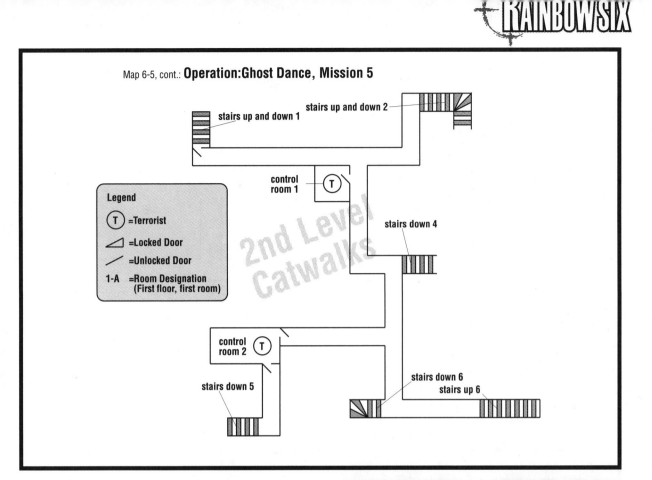

Map 6-5, cont.: **Operation:Ghost Dance, Mission 5**

stairs up and down 1

stairs up and down 2

control
room 1

Legend

(T) =Terrorist

=Locked Door

=Unlocked Door

1-A =Room Designation
(First floor, first room)

2nd Level
Catwalks

stairs down 4

control
room 2

stairs down 5

stairs down 6

stairs up 6

Notes

The key to this mission is timing and stealth. Most of the guards aren't all that alert. Use heartbeat sensors to locate them before entering a room. Don't use frag grenades or flashbangs; they'll only give you away and provoke the tangos to execute the hostages.

This mission uses several Go codes. The first code Alpha orders all four teams to enter the building. The second Alpha sends Blue, Red, and Gold teams into areas where they'll run into tangos. Green Team has a bit farther to travel and so needn't wait for this code. The final code, Delta, is the signal for all teams to converge on tangos with shots at the hostages. While Gold and Red concentrate on the tangos in the room with the hostages, Blue clears the catwalks above and Green secures the control room overlooking the scene.

Fig. 6-32. Red Team leads the hostages from the building and Gold Team follows close behind.

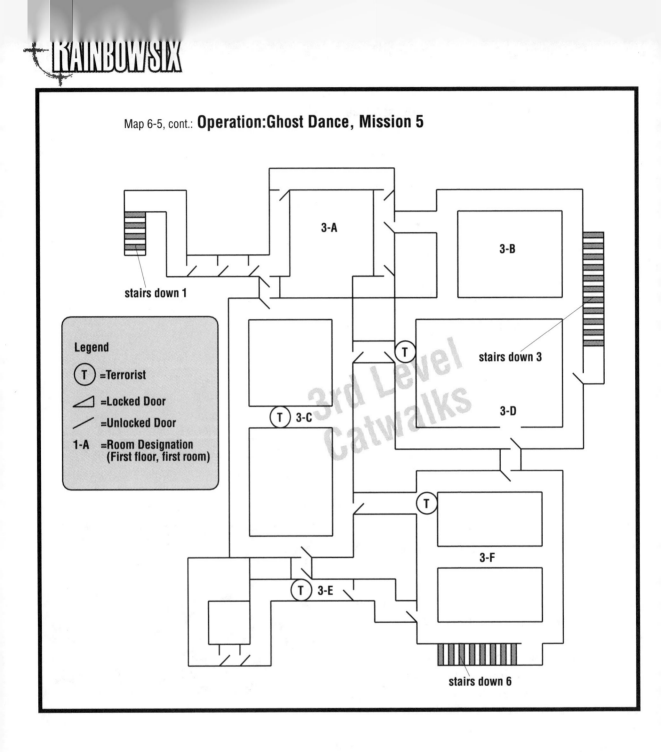

Map 6-5, cont.: **Operation:Ghost Dance, Mission 5**

3-A

3-B

stairs down 1

Legend

(T) =Terrorist

=Locked Door

=Unlocked Door

1-A =Room Designation
(First floor, first room)

stairs down 3

3-C

3-D

3rd Level Catwalks

3-F

3-E

stairs down 6

MISSION 6—OPERATION: BLUE SKY

09.050   **0140**
Hungary

Fig. 6-33. Three bombs have been placed separately, deep within the dam. Your teams must disarm them before the tangos can set them off.

Mission Orders

The Phoenix Group has seized a dam on the border between Hungary and Slovakia and threatens to destroy it. One of the terrorists, a Dutch student named Roland Kunst, will turn informant if you can bring him out alive.

Surveillance indicates that explosive devices have been placed deep inside the dam. If the terrorists learn of the team's presence they'll detonate the devices using triggers scattered throughout the area. Kunst's last communication indicated he's hiding in the dam's upper levels.

Your team will be inserted on the Slovakian side of the river. Two new operatives are assigned to your team for this mission.

Objectives

1. Rescue Roland Kunst.
2. Prevent bomb detonation.

Mission Data

Difficulty Level	Terrorists	Hostages	Other
Recruit	24	1	3 Bombs
Veteran	30	1	3 Bombs
Elite	30	1	3 Bombs

Team Assignments

Blue Team

Operative	Primary	Secondary	Slot 1	Slot 2	Uniform
Chavez	MP5-SD5	.45 Mark-SD	Frag Grenades	Flashbangs	Urban Medium
Yacoby	MP5-SD5	.45 Mark-SD	Frag Grenades	Heartbeat Sensor	Urban Medium

Red Team

Operative	Primary	Secondary	Slot 1	Slot 2	Uniform
Noronha	MP5-SD5	.45 Mark-SD	Frag Grenades	Flashbangs	Urban Medium
Raymond	MP5-SD5	.45 Mark-SD	Frag Grenades	Heartbeat Sensor	Urban Medium

Green Team

Operative	Primary	Secondary	Slot 1	Slot 2	Uniform
Walther	MP5-SD5	.45 Mark-SD	Frag Grenades	Flashbangs	Urban Heavy
Beckenbauer	MP5-SD5	.45 Mark-SD	Heartbeat Sensor	Demolitions Kit	Urban Heavy

Gold Team

Operative	Primary	Secondary	Slot 1	Slot 2	Uniform
Bogart	MP5-SD5	.45 Mark-SD	Frag Grenades	Flashbangs	Urban Heavy
Morris	MP5-SD5	.45 Mark-SD	Heartbeat Sensor	Demolitions Kit	Urban Heavy

Fig. 6-34. Be wary: danger lurks in the stairways. Don't let a tango surprise you.

Strategy

This mission isn't difficult if you plan well. Rescuing Roland Kunst is your top priority. He has valuable information, possibly worth more than the dam itself. However, you also must prevent the terrorists from blowing the dam. To accomplish all this, you'll need four teams. Two teams will defuse the bombs while a third prevents the terrorists from detonating them before they can be disarmed. The final team will get Kunst out of the dam to safety.

The enemy isn't really expecting you, so you have an advantage. Also, the dam consists of long, narrow passageways and tunnels, as well as large rooms. This makes the operation a bit easier, because you can take some long shots.

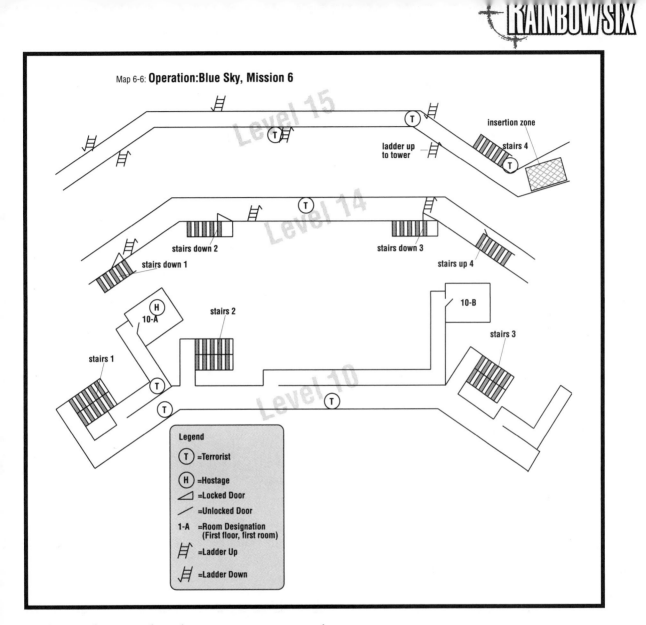

Map 6-6: **Operation:Blue Sky, Mission 6**

Level 15

Level 14

Level 10

insertion zone

stairs 4

ladder up
to tower

stairs down 2

stairs down 3

stairs up 4

stairs down 1

10-B

10-A

stairs 2

stairs 3

stairs 1

Legend

(T) =Terrorist

(H) =Hostage

◢ =Locked Door

╱ =Unlocked Door

1-A =Room Designation
(First floor, first room)

🪜 =Ladder Up

🪜 =Ladder Down

Give each team a heartbeat sensor to prevent the enemy surprising them. Use silenced weapons to prevent triggering an alarm that could lead the terrorists to blow the dam. Once the detonator is secured, however, feel free to use flashbangs and grenades.

Be cautious as you descend the various flights of stairs. Tangos patrol some of them. Often it's a good idea to sidestep the corners so you're not surprised.

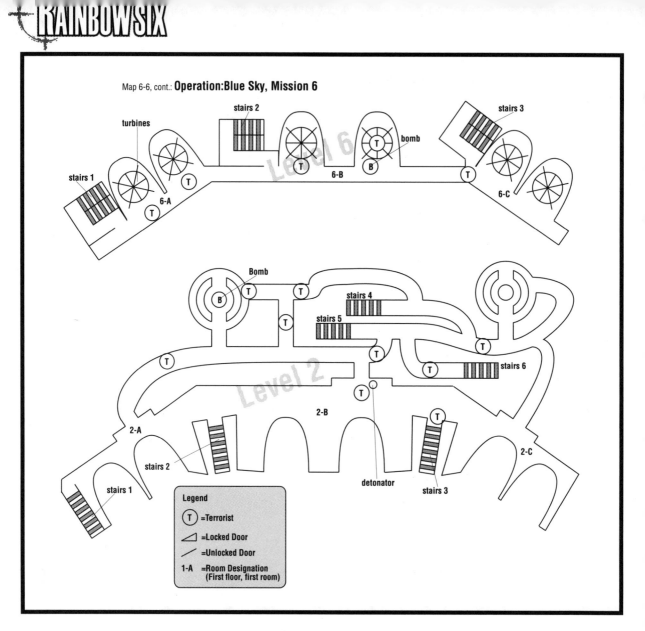

Map 6-6, cont.: **Operation: Blue Sky, Mission 6**

Finally, you needn't get all your operatives out of the dam. After you've gotten Kunst out and disarmed the bombs, the mission ends.

Blue Team

Blue Team is the best team to control. Its job is to get down to the detonator as quickly as possible, and to clear a path for the teams that follow.

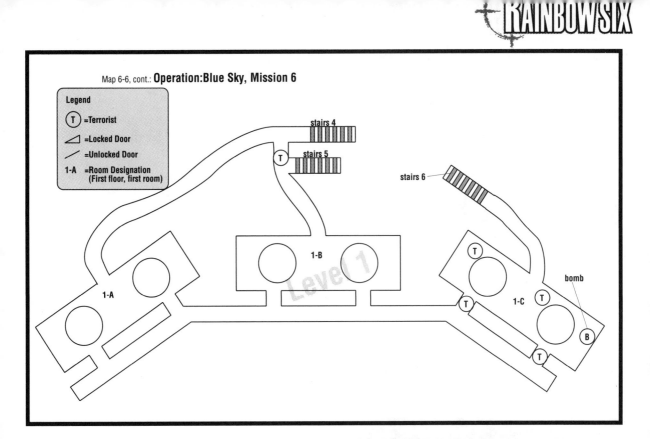

Map 6-6, cont.: **Operation:Blue Sky, Mission 6**

Legend

(T) =Terrorist

◿ =Locked Door

╱ =Unlocked Door

1-A =Room Designation
(First floor, first room)

stairs 4

stairs 5

stairs 6

Level 1

1-B

1-A

1-C

bomb

All teams begin in the tunnel to the dam. Approach the dam carefully. To the right of the tunnel entrance is a small concrete building with a stairway down to the water. Atop the building is a tango. Take him out, as well as another tango at a distance. The door to the stairway is locked, so you'll have to pick it. The stairs take you to level 14. Advance along the pathway to stairway 3. Take out the tango patrolling near the center of the dam. Pick the lock to get through the door and then descend the stairs.

You'll meet at least one tango on the way down. Eliminate him before he can get off a shot. Continue down to level 2 and hold at the stairway for code Alpha. Next, move out into room 2-B and take out the tango near the detonator. There's another tango up on the turbines. Guard the detonator until you receive another Alpha code.

Fig. 6-35. Blue Team clears out one of the large rooms.

Fig. 6-36. Guard the detonator so the tangos can't set off the bombs. The best way to prevent this, however, is to hunt down the tangos in the area.

Your next task is to clear the tunnels on this level, especially those to room 2-D, where a bomb is located. This makes Green Team's job a bit easier. When you've done this, head down stairway 4 to level 1. Now you must clear the way for Gold Team. Go through room 1-B and down the tunnel to 1-C. Hold for code Alpha before you reach the room's first entrance. A tango is stationed at each room entrance and two more wait inside. After you clear the room, your mission ends.

Red Team

Red Team's task is to find Kunst and get him out of the dam. This is the only team for which you must plot an escape. Hold in the tunnel until you receive code Bravo. Then go down stairway 4 to level 14, across the path to stairway 3, and down to level 10. Blue Team has cleared the path to this point. Hold in the stairway for another Bravo code. When it comes, move out into the passage. Two tangos should confront you as you advance down the long corridor to the catwalk leading to room 10-A. A third waits on the catwalk. The heartbeat sensor will tell you what's around the corners. From the catwalk, you can see levels 2 and 6. Feel free to take out any tangos you can get in your sights.

Fig. 6-37. Kunst's information about the Phoenix Group is more precious than the dam and his safety is your main objective.

You'll find Kunst in room 10-A. Escort him as quickly as possible to the extraction zone in the tunnel. Follow the same route you took into the dam and you should have no trouble. Wait in the tunnel for the other teams to complete their assignments.

Green Team

Disarming two of the bombs is Green Team's task. Be sure this team includes a demolitions specialist with a demolitions kit. Hold in the tunnel for code Charlie, and then follow Blue Team's path down to level 6, using stairway 3. Hold in the stairway for a second code Charlie. Then move out into the passageway toward area 6-B. The bomb is next to the turbine nearest you. Before disarming it, take out the tango patrolling the area, as well as another one standing on the turbine.

After disarming the first bomb, walk to stairway 2 and descend to level 2. Hold in the stairway until you get another Charlie code. Now advance quickly through area 2-A to room 2-D. You'll encounter a few tangos along the way, but Blue Team should have cleared most of them for you. Disarm the second bomb and then wait for Gold Team to take care of the third. Your mission is over.

Fig. 6-38. Take out the tango guarding the bomb near the turbine. Use Sniper view to get a good aim at long range.

Gold Team

Gold Team is the other bomb team. Hold in the tunnel for code Delta. Then advance down stairway 3, following Blue Team's path, to level 2. Hold for another code Delta, and then make your way to stairway 6. Descend to level 1 and wait outside room 1-C for the third Delta code. You'll get it after Blue Team clears the room for you. Then enter and disarm the bomb there. If the other bombs were disarmed and Kunst taken to safety, your mission should end.

Fig. 6-39. Disarm the last bomb to complete the mission.

Notes

For this mission, you need control only Blue Team. The computer can run the other three teams successfully if you plan well. While the other three teams hold in the tunnel, Blue Team clears a path to stairway 3 on level 14, and then takes out tangos on the way down to level 2. Once you're in the stairway, give codes Bravo, Charlie, and Delta, with about 10 seconds between them, so the three teams won't get stuck in the stairway. When Red Team awaits Bravo, give the code so they can begin their rescue of Kunst. You need no longer concern yourself with that objective.

Fig. 6-40. Four tangos guard the final bomb. The last is right next to it.

Note

If a demolitions team can't complete its task, you can control the other team and manually disarm their assigned bombs.

As soon as Blue Team reaches level 2, go ahead and give code Alpha; then you can secure the detonator. Give code Charlie to Green Team so they can advance to disarm bomb 2 on level 6. When they finish, they'll continue down to level 2 via stairway 2. As they disarm the first bomb, Blue Team can begin clearing the tunnels on level 2.

By the time Green Team is holding for Charlie, the path will be safer for them and for Gold Team. Give both codes Charlie and Delta, and then take Blue Team down to level 1 to clear out room 1-C for Gold Team. Next, give the final Delta code and wait for Gold Team to disarm the last bomb and complete the mission.

MISSION 7—OPERATION: FIRE WALK

09.10.00   0700
Idaho

Fig. 6-41. The leaders will try to make a break for the HMV. Kill them before they can escape with the biological agents.

Mission Orders

The Phoenix Group is operating a secret biological warfare installation in southern Idaho. The team must secure the compound with minimal casualties. Lethal biological agents may be present within the main laboratory building. Breach of biosuit integrity in this environment may result in death.

You'll be inserted over the wall in the rear of the compound. If they detect your presence, Phoenix members carrying virus samples will try to escape through the front gate, so secure this area first.

IF YOU ALLOW ANYONE TO LEAVE THE COMPOUND, YOUR MISSION FAILS.

Intelligence indicates the compound's occupants won't expect an attack. They probably will be unarmed, offering little resistance.

Objectives

1. Kill all terrorists.
2. Prevent both leaders from leaving.

Mission Data

Difficulty Level	Terrorists	Hostages	Other
Recruit	12	0	1 HMV
Veteran	20	0	1 HMV
Elite	27	0	1 HMV

Team Assignments

Blue Team

Operative	Primary	Secondary	Slot 1	Slot 2	Uniform
Hanley	CAR-15	.45 Mark 23	Frag Grenades	Frag Grenades	Biosuit
Raymond	CAR-15	.45 Mark 23	Frag Grenades	Heartbeat Sensor	Biosuit

Red Team

Operative	Primary	Secondary	Slot 1	Slot 2	Uniform
Burke	CAR-15	.45 Mark 23	Frag Grenades	Frag Grenades	Biosuit
Sweeney	CAR-15	.45 Mark 23	Frag Grenades	Heartbeat Sensor	Biosuit

Green Team

Operative	Primary	Secondary	Slot 1	Slot 2	Uniform
Arnavisca	M-16A2	.45 Mark 23	Frag Grenades	Frag Grenades	Wood Heavy
Maldini	M-16A2	.45 Mark 23	Frag Grenades	Heartbeat Sensor	Wood Heavy

Gold Team

Operative	Primary	Secondary	Slot 1	Slot 2	Uniform
Woo	M-16A2	.45 Mark 23	Frag Grenades	Frag Grenades	Wood Heavy
Yacoby	M-16A2	.45 Mark 23	Frag Grenades	Heartbeat Sensor	Wood Heavy

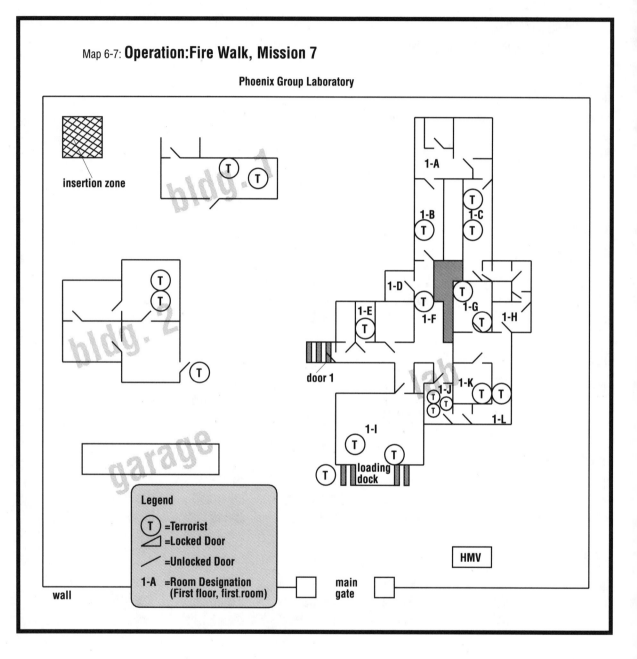

Map 6-7: **Operation:Fire Walk, Mission 7**

Phoenix Group Laboratory

insertion zone

bldg. 1

bldg. 2

garage

lab

door 1

1-A

1-B

1-C

1-D

1-E

1-F

1-G

1-H

1-I

1-J

1-K

1-L

loading dock

Legend

(T) =Terrorist

◹ =Locked Door

╱ =Unlocked Door

1-A =Room Designation (First floor, first room)

wall

main gate

HMV

Strategy

This is a tough mission. The briefing states that you're unexpected and can take the camp without firing a shot. That intelligence is extremely faulty. Not only will the tangos fight back, but they all wear body armor. You must pull out the heavy artillery. All your operatives should carry either the CAR-15 or the M-16A2. These will give you a bit more punch than the MP5 models. The silenced submachine gun would be nice, but the surprise would be short-lived.

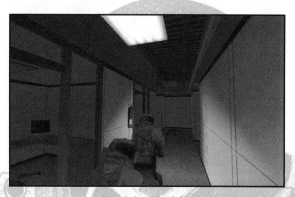

Fig. 6-42. The lab contains dangerous biological agents. All operatives entering the lab must wear biosuits.

This mission requires four teams. Although the briefing doesn't state it, another mission follows immediately after this one. Because it follows up in the same area, you must use the same operatives, so choose good ones. Those you used in the last mission may be fatigued, lowering their abilities. Be sure to take eight operatives: you don't know what you'll be up against in the next mission.

One of the mission's four teams will cover the main gate to prevent escapes. The second team will clear the two smaller buildings. The remaining two teams will enter the lab and kill everyone inside. Because the lab contains dangerous biological agents, all operatives who enter it must wear biosuits. These are not very protective against bullets and a puncture can mean death. Therefore, you must exercise great caution inside the lab. Use heartbeat sensors to locate hiding tangos. Throw frag grenades as much as possible to kill tangos around corners.

Blue Team

Blue Team is your main lab infiltrator. Advance next to building 1 and hold for Alpha code. Then move up to door 1 of the lab and wait for a second Alpha. This is the go to enter the lab. There's a tango in room 1-E. Throw a frag grenade around the corner to take him out. Then wait for other tangos to come and investigate. The heartbeat sensor enables you to see them before they

Fig. 6-43. Blue Team must move through decontaminating rooms with spray to find and kill all the terrorists.

come into visual range. Mow them down with your rifles as you await a third Alpha.

Throw a frag grenade into 1-J to take out the tango hiding behind the locker; then advance toward 1-B. A tango is stationed in 1-D, but he probably was killed in the hallway when he came to see what was happening. The same goes for the tango in 1-B. (He may be there or you may have killed him already.) Continue around to 1-A, and then through the disinfecting spray to 1-C. Here you'll find one or two tangos. Dispatch them quickly with a frag grenade or full-automatic bursts. Advance to room 1-H and hold for Alpha. There are two tangos in 1-G. Sidestep out of 1-H, shoot out the glass window of 1-G, and throw in a frag grenade. Carefully approach room 1-K and do the same to the tango inside. A final tango waits in hall 1-L. Kill him and exit the lab.

Fig. 6-44. Throw frag grenades at tangos hidden behind corners or lockers.

Red Team

Red Team is the other team to enter the lab and so needs protective biosuits. At the beginning, head to the compound's northeast corner, and then advance down the other side of the lab until you have a view of the loading dock from the side. Wait there for code Bravo. Shoot any tangos that come out of the loading dock before they can escape in the HMV.

When you receive code Bravo, enter the loading area (1-I) and hold in the doorway to hall 1-F for another Bravo code. Shoot any tangos that come into your sights. Use the heartbeat sensor to monitor tangos out of your visual range. When you get the next code, advance to room 1-J, careful to take out any tangos hiding in there. Pause there until you get yet another Bravo. Enter room 1-L through the spray room and take out the tango there. You can take out the tango in 1-K through the window, as well. Use caution when rounding the corner: the two tangos in room 1-G will have a shot at you. Take them out and wait for Blue Team to meet up with you.

Green Team

Green Team's task is to clear the other two buildings in the compound. Advance down the west wall past building 2. Turn east to take out a tango next to the lab loading dock. Hold for code Charlie. Another tango patrols the center of the compound. Drop him as he comes into view. Using the heartbeat sensor, locate the two tangos in building 2 before entering. If they're not in the first room when you enter, then throw frag grenades through the doorways to kill them where they hide.

When the building is clear, head to building 1. One of the tangos may have come out the door to investigate the gunshots. Drop him. Otherwise, use caution as you approach the door and when you open it. Throw a frag grenade into the corner of the room where the tangos are, and then rush in to finish the job. You can also try throwing a grenade through the window. Hold outside building 1 and cover door 1 of the lab in case any tangos try to escape.

Gold Team

Gold Team covers the main gate to prevent tango leaders from escaping with biological agents. Advance down the west wall to the south corner; then move east to the edge of the garage, where you have a good view of the loading dock, the HMV, and the area between. This is your killing ground. Shoot any tangos in this area to prevent their escape. That is all you have to do in this mission.

Notes

You should begin in control of Green Team. The two small buildings must be cleared before Blue Team approaches the lab, because the tangos in these buildings can fire through the windows at your operatives. Give Charlie codes so Green can clear building 2, and

Fig. 6-45. The tangos in room 1-G have a clear shot down the hallway. Either shoot them first or shoot out the window and throw in a frag grenade to eliminate them.

Fig. 6-46. Green Team clears building 1.

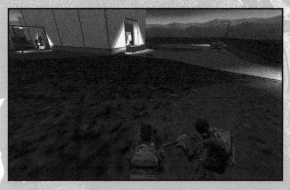

Fig. 6-47. Gold Team covers the main gate to make sure no one escapes from the compound.

then building 1. Gold Team automatically will go to its post and take out any tangos attempting to leave. Red Team also has a good field of fire into this area from the other side of the lab. When Green Team finishes its job, give code Alpha for Blue Team to approach door 1 of the lab.

Now take control of Blue. You can do a better job than the computer for this next difficult task. Give code Alpha again to enter the lab. Code Bravo tells Red Team to enter the lab through the loading dock. Together, you should be able to catch several tangos in a cross fire. Once Blue Team clears 1-F and 1-J, give Red another Bravo code and have them wait in 1-J while you take Blue Team through the rest of the lab.

This mission leads into the next. Any operatives wounded or fatigued in this mission will remain so in the next. Therefore, it is imperative you keep your people safe and healthy.

Fig. 6-48. Inside the lab, you'll find humans being used as test subjects for deadly biological weapons.

MISSION 8—OPERATION: WINTER HAWK

09.10.00   0600
Idaho

Mission Orders

Leaders of the Phoenix Group's Idaho operation have fled to a local airstrip. They're believed to carry dangerous biological agents and probably will attempt to leave the area by airplane.

You'll approach the airstrip from behind the control tower.

Time constraints limit you to the team employed on the preceding mission.

Objectives

1. Kill all terrorists.
2. Prevent both leaders from escaping in the plane.

Mission Data

Difficulty Level	Terrorists	Leaders	Other
Recruit	10	1	1 plane
Veteran	11	2	2 planes
Elite	14	4	2 planes

Team Assignments

Blue Team

Operative	Primary	Secondary	Slot 1	Slot 2	Uniform
Hanley	CAR-15	.45 Mark 23	Frag Grenade	Frag Grenade	Wood Heavy
Raymond	CAR-15	.45 Mark 23	Frag Grenade	Heartbeat Sensor	Wood Heavy

Red Team

Operative	Primary	Secondary	Slot 1	Slot 2	Uniform
Burke	CAR-15	.45 Mark 23	Frag Grenade	Frag Grenade	Wood Heavy
Sweeney	CAR-15	.45 Mark 23	Frag Grenade	Heartbeat Sensor	Wood Heavy

Green Team

Operative	Primary	Secondary	Slot 1	Slot 2	Uniform
Arnavisca	CAR-15	.45 Mark 23	Frag Grenade	Frag Grenade	Wood Heavy
Maldini	CAR-15	.45 Mark 23	Frag Grenade	Heartbeat Sensor	Wood Heavy

Gold Team

Operative	Primary	Secondary	Slot 1	Slot 2	Uniform
Woo	CAR-15	.45 Mark 23	Frag Grenade	Frag Grenade	Wood Heavy
Yacoby	CAR-15	.45 Mark 23	Frag Grenade	Heartbeat Sensor	Wood Heavy

Fig. 6-49. You must kill both leaders before they can escape in the business jet.

Fig. 6-50. Take out the terrorist in room 1-A with a long-range shot through the window.

Fig. 6-51. Take care when taking out the leader. He's armed with a pistol.

Strategy

Strategy for this mission is fairly simple, but the execution can be tough, due to the wide-open airfield and large hangars. Two of your teams must cover the airfield to prevent the Phoenix Group leaders' escape. The leaders wear white lab coats and will try to escape as soon as they hear shooting. Kill them quickly. If they reach either the Hawker business jet or the Cessna, the planes will take off with them. The other two teams must clear the hangars and the airport building. Use all the frag grenades you want: you must kill all tangos to complete this mission.

Blue Team

Blue Team must clear the building. This is the toughest task, so you should do it yourself. From the insertion zone, move east to the northeast corner of hangar 1. Wait for Alpha, and then run toward door 1 of the building. You should be able to shoot through a rear window and take out a tango inside room 1-A or in the hall. Open the door and rush in. There are one or two tangos in the front room (1-D). Throw a frag grenade around the corner to take them out. The leader is in room 1-C, if he hasn't tried to get away already. He has a pistol, so use caution in killing him. One last tango waits upstairs. He has a good field of view over the airfield, so you must take him out before your other teams can operate in the open. Carefully ascend the stairs and drop him.

Red Team

Red Team's job is to clear hangar 1. At the start, advance to position the team just around the corner from door 1. At Alpha, rush into the hangar and take out the two tangos—one on each side of the plane. If you see only one, the other may be

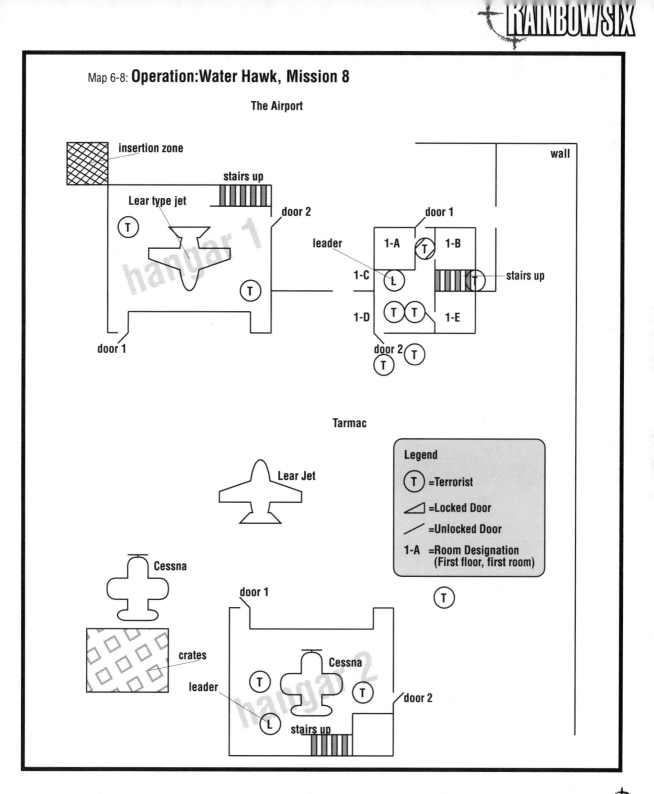

Map 6-8: Operation:Water Hawk, Mission 8

The Airport

insertion zone

wall

stairs up

Lear type jet

door 2

door 1

hangar 1

leader

1-A

1-B

1-C

stairs up

door 1

1-D

1-E

door 2

Tarmac

Legend

(T) =Terrorist

=Locked Door

=Unlocked Door

1-A =Room Designation
(First floor, first room)

Lear Jet

Cessna

door 1

crates

Cessna

leader

hangar 2

door 2

stairs up

Fig. 6-52. Red Team must clear hangar 1. It holds only two terrorists, but the large building can be a deathtrap if you're not careful.

Fig. 6-53. Green Team can cover door 2 of the airport building and shoot anybody who tries to make a break for the planes.

Fig. 6-54. Gold Team enters hangar 2 to clear it.

up on the catwalk above the plane. When the hangar is clear, exit through door 2 and run to the building. Take up a position around the corner from door 2. From there you can cover the Hawker business jet on the tarmac and prevent the group leaders from reaching it.

Green Team

Green Team's task is to cover the airport building and prevent anyone from reaching the Hawker business jet. At the beginning, move to a spot around the corner from door 1 of hangar 1. Cautiously advance to the other side of the large hangar door at code Alpha. From there, shoot any tangos out on the tarmac in front of the airport building and any tangos headed for the planes. Hold this position until you receive code Charlie.

Then run to door 2 of hangar 2. At code Delta, throw in a frag grenade, and then rush in to clear the room of tangos. There are two inside, along with a leader, if he hasn't tried to escape already.

Gold Team

Gold Team must cover the airfield's south side and prevent anyone from escaping in the Cessna outside hangar 2. At the beginning of the mission, run south toward the Cessna to a point near the container. At Alpha, approach door 1 of hangar 2. Hold several meters from the door. Kill any exiting tangos, as well as any you can see on the tarmac. At code Delta, throw a frag grenade in door 1 of the hangar and enter to clear it out. Use caution: Green Team will enter the hangar from the other door.

Notes

The key to this mission is to cover the airfield and prevent any leader's escape. Do this, and you can take your time mopping up the tangos. You should only have to control Blue Team; the others can manage on their own if they get good orders during planning.

At the beginning of the mission, all teams move into their jump-off positions. Give code Alpha and Red Team will rush hangar 1, while Green and Gold Team move to where they can cover the two aircraft. After Red Team clears the hangar and takes up a position covering the tarmac and door 2 of the airport building, give code Charlie and send Green Team to help clear hangar 2. At code Delta, both Green and Gold will rush the hangar.

Although rushing all the buildings is an active strategy, you also can take a passive course of action for the mission's first half: Kill all the tangos outside the buildings and cover the doors. When the leaders or other tangos come out to investigate or escape, take them down. Then mop up stragglers in the buildings. By now, few tangos will remain, and your breaches will be safer.

Fig. 6-55. Gold and Green teams work together to clear hangar 2.

MISSION 9—OPERATION: RED WOLF

09.13.00   1500
Brussels

Mission Orders

Members of a British neo-Nazi terrorist organization have seized control of the central European mint during a celebration honoring the first production run of the new European currency. They hold several dignitaries hostage in the mint's vault.

Belgian authorities have cordoned off the area. You'll be inserted near the mint's main gate. Return there after you free the hostages.

Your team has two new operatives for this mission.

Objective

1. Rescue all hostages.

Mission Data

Difficulty Level	Terrorists	Hostages	Other
Recruit	9	3	None
Veteran	13	3	None
Elite	17	3	None

Team Assignments

Blue Team

Operative	Primary	Secondary	Slot 1	Slot 2	Uniform
Chavez	MP5SD5	.45 Mark SD	Frag Grenades	Flashbangs	Black Medium
Arnavisca	MP5SD5	.45 Mark SD	Frag Grenades	Heartbeat Sensor	Black Medium

Red Team

Operative	Primary	Secondary	Slot 1	Slot 2	Uniform
Walther	MP5SD5	.45 Mark SD	Frag Grenades	Flashbangs	Black Medium
Maldini	MP5SD5	.45 Mark SD	Frag Grenades	Heartbeat Sensor	Black Medium

Fig. 6-56. You must rescue the dignitaries the neo-Nazis hold hostage in this Belgian mint.

Strategy

This is a tough mission. Although there aren't that many tangos, they're positioned to ambush infiltrators. You could complete this entire mission with only one team, but it's better (and safer) to use two, due to the physical structure of the pressing room, where the money is printed: The second floor, which forms the ceiling of the first, is made up of steel bars. Tangos at the top can fire down at your team, or, if you're on top, enemies below can fire up at you. Therefore, one team must clear the bottom while the other clears the top. The first team will enter through

Map 6-9: **Operation:Red Wolf, Mission 9**

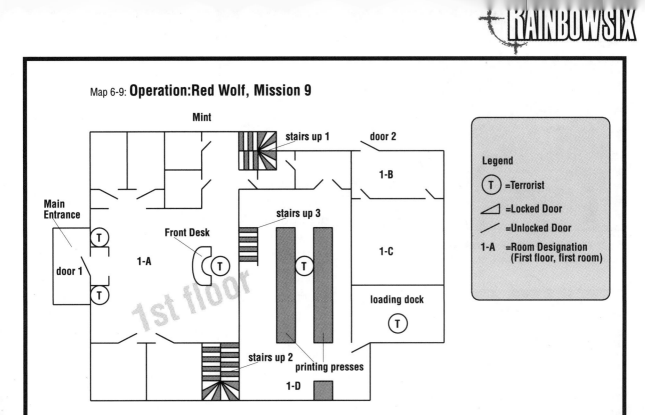

Mint

stairs up 1

door 2

1-B

Main
Entrance

door 1

Front Desk

stairs up 3

1-C

1-A

loading dock

1st floor

stairs up 2

printing presses

1-D

Legend

(T) =Terrorist

◁ =Locked Door

╱ =Unlocked Door

1-A =Room Designation
(First floor, first room)

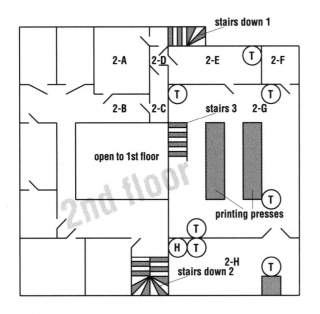

stairs down 1

2-A 2-D 2-E 2-F

2-B 2-C stairs 3 2-G

open to 1st floor

2nd floor

printing presses

2-H

stairs down 2

Fig. 6-57. The floor of the second level of the pressing room can be seen (and fired) through.

Fig. 6-58. Use Sniper view to take out the guard on the loading dock. He may look like a security guard, but he's really a terrorist.

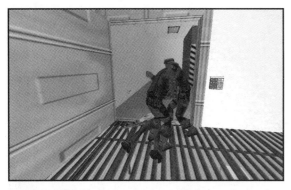

Fig. 6-59. Blue Team prepares to enter the room containing the hostages. They must shoot quickly and carefully to avoid hitting a hostage. Use three-round bursts to keep your shots on target.

the front and clear a path for the second team, which will go in and rescue the hostages.

Blue Team

Blue Team enters the mint through door 2 on the side. This is your hostage rescue team. Hold at the door for code Alpha. Enter room 1-B, and then 1-C. A tango dressed like a security guard patrols the loading dock. Take him out before entering the room. Advance to the loading dock and hold by the door to 1-D until you receive another code Alpha. Then rush into the room. Take out the single tango on this floor and any on the next level you can see through the ceiling. Take care not to shoot at Red Team, which is clearing the level above you at the same time.

Climb stairway 3, and then walk to the doorway to 2-H. Wait for another Alpha code. Next, take out the tango close to the door; then sidestep in to take out the second tango before he can shoot the hostages. You must act quickly and shoot carefully. Use Sniper view for better aim. Fire only a three-round burst or the spread may hit the hostages. Run to the hostages, escort them from the mint the way you entered, and return to the extraction zone.

Red Team

Red Team must clear the second floor of the pressing room for Blue Team. To get there, they must enter through the front door. Hold at door 1 for code Bravo. Use the heartbeat sensor to see where the tangos are positioned inside the first room. Then open the door and carefully move inside. Take out the guard standing behind or to one side of the front desk. Another tango waits on the balcony above. Be careful about moving out in the open until you've killed her.

Two more guards, one on either side of the entrance, may come to you if they hear a shot or see one of their number go down. Shoot them as they round the corner to the entrance. If they stay put, you must go to them. Throw a frag grenade around the corner to take out one. That will alert the other. Turn and take him down before he can get off a shot.

With the four tangos in the front part of the mint dead, head for stairway 1. Ascend to the second floor, and then go through rooms 2-A, 2-B, and 2-C to reach the door to 2-D. A tango at the end of 2-E looks right at the doorway. Throw a frag grenade around the corner. When it goes off, rush in, shooting. If the frag grenade doesn't kill the tango, it will stun him, at least, and get you through the doorway to drop him with your submachine gun.

Quickly move to room 2-F. Sidestep to the doorway to take out the two tangos along the outer wall. You must get the one next to the doorway to room 2-H. He'll run into the hostage room, if you let him, making the rescue more difficult. Two more guards patrol the other wall. Take them down, and then wait for Blue Team to come upstairs and rescue the hostages. On their way out, give code Bravo and run out after them to protect their rear as they leave.

Notes

Control Red Team. Reaching the second floor is tricky. The first Bravo code gives you the go to enter the front doors, the second to advance into the lobby. Give Blue Team the Alpha code to enter the back door as you go in the front. Give another Bravo code before taking out the guard in room 2-E. Once this room is clear, give code Alpha so Blue team will enter the first floor of the pressing

Fig. 6-60. Take out the guard at the other end of the lobby. This time he's off to one side with his back turned. Take him out before he knows what's happening.

Fig. 6-61. The guard at the far end of room 2-E waits to ambush your team. Throw a frag grenade around the corner, and then rush in, guns blazing.

Fig. 6-62. If you don't act fast enough as you enter the hostage room, the tango will begin executing them.

room as you clear the top. Another Alpha code brings them up the stairs while you hold for a Bravo. The final Alpha sends Blue in to get the hostages. Chavez is a good shot and will be sure to hit the terrorist and not the hostages. Give the last Bravo code as Blue heads down the stairs and get both teams to safety along with the hostages.

If you feel like a challenge, play this mission as a single operative. Follow Blue Team's path. However, in the pressing room, take out all the second-floor guards from below. Watch out for the guard in room 2-E. He has a shot at you as you come up the stairs.

MISSION 10—OPERATION: RAZOR ICE

09.19.00   2300
Southampton

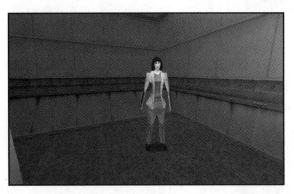

Fig. 6-63. Dr. Winston is in the engine room, on the ship's first level.

Mission Orders

Members of the Phoenix Group have kidnapped Dr. Catherine Winston and taken her to a ship anchored in Southampton Harbor. The harbor patrol has blockaded the vessel to prevent it from sailing, but Phoenix members have a bomb onboard and threaten to destroy the ship if they're not allowed to leave.

Surveillance indicates they hold Dr. Winston in the engine room. No intelligence is available for the location of the explosive device. Given your limited time, you should make no effort to find it. During your assault, make certain none of the hostiles raises the alarm. The group leader has barricaded himself in the bow of the ship and will trigger the bomb if he learns of your presence.

Your team will be inserted by inflatable boat at the stern of the ship. Rendezvous there for extraction after you achieve your objective.

Objective
1. Rescue Dr. Winston

Mission Data

Difficulty Level	Terrorists	Hostages	Other
Recruit	12	1	1 Bomb
Veteran	19	1	1 Bomb
Elite	22	1	1 Bomb

Team Assignments

Blue Team

Operative	Primary	Secondary	Slot 1	Slot 2	Uniform
Chavez	MP5SD5	.45 Mark SD	Empty	Empty	Urban Medium
Filatov	MP5SD5	.45 Mark SD	Heartbeat Sensor	Empty	Urban Medium

Red Team

Operative	Primary	Secondary	Slot 1	Slot 2	Uniform
Hanley	MP5SD5	.45 Mark SD	Empty	Empty	Urban Medium
Rakuzanka	MP5SD5	.45 Mark SD	Heartbeat Sensor	Empty	Urban Medium

Green Team

Operative	Primary	Secondary	Slot 1	Slot 2	Uniform
Walther	MP5SD5	.45 Mark SD	Empty	Empty	Urban Breach
Raymond	MP5SD5	.45 Mark SD	Heartbeat Sensor	Empty	Urban Breach

Gold Team

Operative	Primary	Secondary	Slot 1	Slot 2	Uniform
Bogart	MP5SD5	.45 Mark SD	Empty	Empty	Urban Breach
Arnavisca	MP5SD5	.45 Mark SD	Heartbeat Sensor	Empty	Urban Breach

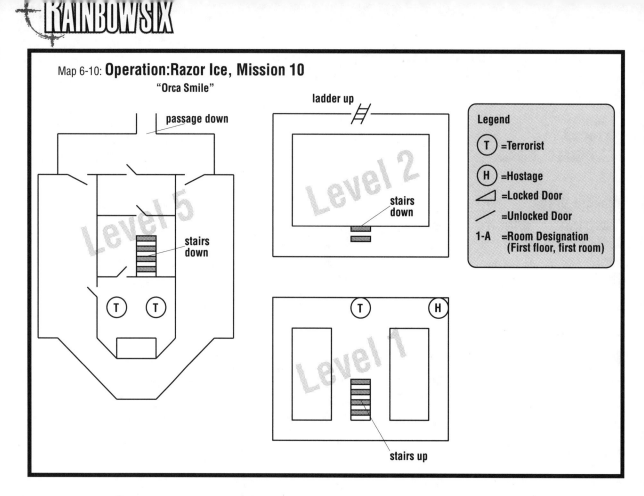

Map 6-10: **Operation:Razor Ice, Mission 10**
"Orca Smile"

passage down

Level 5

stairs
down

T T

ladder up

Level 2

stairs
down

Legend

(T) =Terrorist

(H) =Hostage

◹ =Locked Door

／ =Unlocked Door

1-A =Room Designation
(First floor, first room)

T H

Level 1

stairs up

Strategy

There are a lot of tangos on this ship, but you needn't kill them all to complete the mission. In fact, avoid them as much as possible so they don't alert their leader, who will detonate the bomb and blow up the ship. Don't waste time looking for the explosive; by the time you find it, the leader will have set it off. You need only get down to the engine room, and then escort Dr. Winston to safety.

You'll need four teams. One will rescue Dr. Winston. The others will clear part of the path for the rescue team and cover their route of egress. Stay as stealthy as possible, using silenced weapons only; leave all grenades behind. Each team also should carry a heartbeat sensor. The cramped quarters make ambushes deadly threats. Use the sensor to locate tangos before they find you.

Map 6-10, cont.: **Operation:Razor Ice, Mission 10**

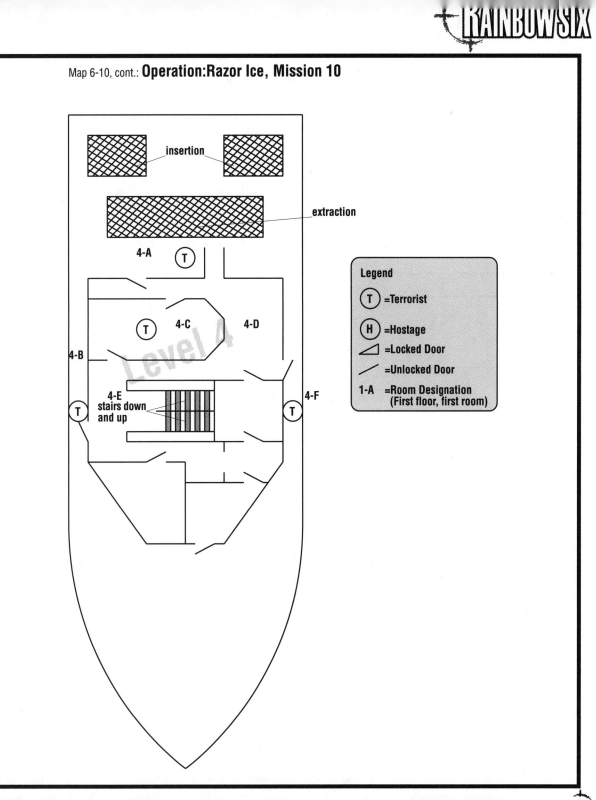

Legend

(T) =Terrorist

(H) =Hostage

◿ =Locked Door

╱ =Unlocked Door

1-A =Room Designation
(First floor, first room)

Map 6-10, cont.: **Operation:Razor Ice, Mission 10**

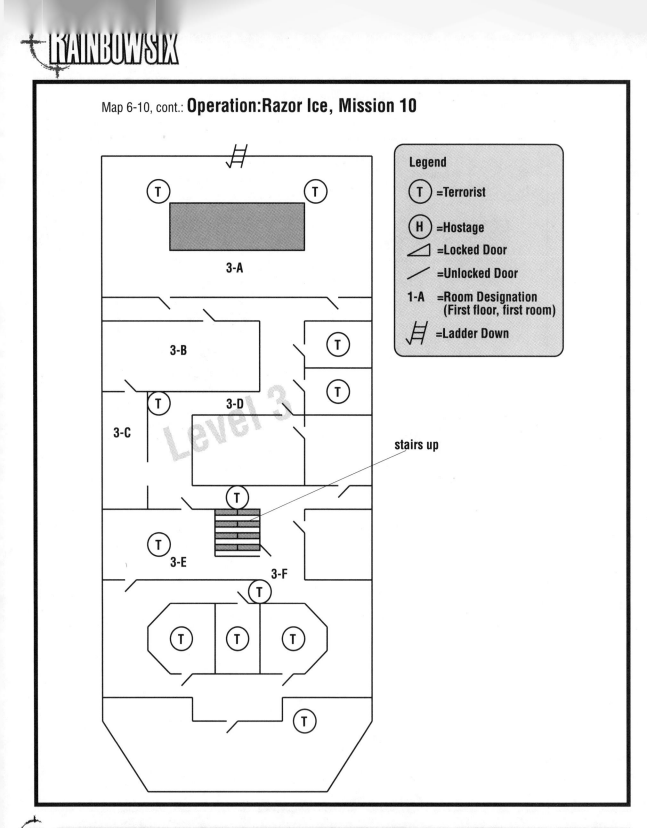

Legend

(T) =Terrorist

(H) =Hostage

=Locked Door

=Unlocked Door

1-A =Room Designation
(First floor, first room)

=Ladder Down

3-A

3-B

3-C

3-D

stairs up

3-E

3-F

Level 3

Blue Team

Blue Team is the rescue team and the one you should control. All teams begin on level 4, near the stern of the ship. There's a tango near area 4-A. Take her out (if another team doesn't beat you to it). Wait at 4-A for Alpha, and then follow Gold Team down passage 4-B to room 4-E. There's a tango in the passage, but Gold will take care of him.

Fig. 6-64. Take care going around corners. Tangos wait to kill you.

Hold for another Alpha in 4-E before continuing downstairs to the third level. Wait for a final Alpha at 3-F. When Gold and Green teams are in position and awaiting code Delta, rush down the passage to 3-C, through 3-B, and into 3-A. Two tangos stand near the ladder at the rear of the room. Carefully sidestep from behind a crate and drop them both with a burst of automatic fire. Move to the ladder down to level 2. A tango on level 1 has a view to the bottom of the ladder, so instead of descending the rungs, grab the sides and slide down quickly. (Just step off the edge. It may seem like falling, but a trained operative wouldn't fall.) This way you arrive at the bottom in a hurry and can bring up your submachine gun to take out the tango on the level below.

Follow the catwalk around to the stairs and descend to level 1, the engine room. Find Dr. Winston and escort her out the way you came. Once you get up the stairs to level 4, give code Delta. This orders the other three teams to leave their positions and make their way to the extraction zone.

Red Team

Red Team's job is to secure level 4 and keep it safe for evacuating the hostage. At the beginning of the mission, run out into area 4-A. Take out the tango there if no one else has. At code Alpha, dash down passage 4-F to take out the tango there, and then make your way to 4-E. Cover the stairway against roaming tangos who may try to sneak up on the other teams. Hold there until code Delta; then make your way to the extraction zone.

Tip

The terrorist leader is in the bow compartment of the ship on level 3. Stay out of there. He stands next to the bomb and will blow up the ship if you come in sight or if he hears nearby gunfire. You can accomplish the mission without disarming the bomb or killing the leader, so don't take this risk.

Fig. 6-65. You can kill the tango guarding Dr. Winston from the base of the ladder on level 2. Take her out before she has a chance to shoot you or execute the doctor.

Fig. 6-66. The tangos on this ship are well-armed with automatic weapons. Red Team must secure level 4 and keep it safe for the hostage evacuation.

Green Team

Green Team is one of the guard teams for level 4. Hold at 4-A until you receive Alpha. Then make your way into room 4-C to take out the tango there. Continue to the stairway and down to level 3. Hold position at 3-F and shoot any patrolling tangos who venture into your line of sight. You must prevent tangos in the ship's bow from getting to the hostage rescue team. Stay here until you receive code Delta, and then make your way back up the stairs to the extraction zone.

Gold Team

Gold Team is the third security team. At Alpha, dash down passage 4-B, taking out the tango on patrol, on into 4-E, and down the stairs to level 3.

Continue toward the stern, clearing a path to area 3-D in the corner of the passage. You'll run into at least one tango as you advance. You must cover the passage and kill any tangos who enter it. There are tangos in the two rooms to the right, but don't risk going in after them: wait for them to come out, and then kill them. Hold at 3-D until you get code Delta. This gives you permission to leave the third level and make your way to the extraction zone, following the path you took on your way in.

Fig. 6-67. Green Team is positioned to keep tangos in the forward part of the ship from interfering with the operation. Shoot anyone who comes into view.

Notes

All teams start at the stern of the ship and advance immediately to area 4-A. Give code Alpha to send all four teams on their way. The three security teams—Red, Green, and Gold—will move to their posts, clearing a path as they go, and hold while Blue Team goes after Dr. Winston. Blue Team will wait on level 4 while the security teams advance. Give an Alpha code again to send Blue Team down to the third level and on to rescue the doctor. Once you're back at level 4 with the hostage, give code Delta and the security teams will head back to the extraction zone.

For this mission, you should control Blue Team. Its task requires some precise tactics. The computer can handle the other three teams just fine, as long as you provide detailed instructions during the planning phase. The key to success in this mission is to stay quiet and take out only those tangos in your way. Remember, the objective is to rescue Dr. Winston, not to wipe out all tangos on the ship.

Fig. 6-68. Gold Team covers the center of the ship from location 3-D, with orders to kill any tangos who enter the area to prevent them getting to the hostage rescue team.

Note

This is another great level for multiplayer games. The narrow passages and small compartments make it ideal for setting up ambushes. In room 4-A, the crates near the ladder have a small gap you can climb into. Lie in wait there for other players to pass by on their way to the ladder.

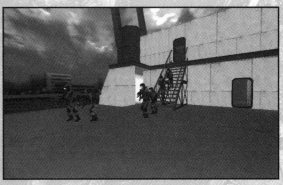

Fig. 6-69. The security teams return to the extraction zone after receiving code Delta.

MISSION 11—OPERATION: YELLOW KNIFE

09.23.00   0800
Alexandria

Fig. 6-70. Five security guards protect Anne Lang's home. If they spot you, the mission fails.

Mission Orders

Information provided by Dr. Winston links Presidential Science Advisor Anne Lang to the Phoenix Group. By bugging Lang's home phone, RAINBOW may gain valuable information about Phoenix's plans.

Lang lives in a walled estate outside Alexandria, Virginia. Armed guards patrol the grounds. The team must enter and leave the compound undetected to gather useful intelligence.

You'll be inserted over the wall at the back of Lang's property and extracted from the same location.

Your team has two new operatives for this mission.

USE OF DEADLY FORCE IS NOT SANCTIONED ON THIS MISSION.

Objective

1. Deactivate security.
2. Bug upstairs phone.
3. Bug downstairs phone.
4. Get to extraction zone.

Mission Data

Difficulty Level	Terrorists	Hostages	Other
Recruit	5	0	1 Bug
Veteran	6	0	2 Bugs
Elite	8	0	2 Bugs

Team Assignments

Blue Team

Operative	Primary	Secondary	Slot 1	Slot 2	Uniform
Lofquist	MP5SD5	.45 Mark SD	Heartbeat Sensor	Electronics Kit	Black Light

Red Team

Operative	Primary	Secondary	Slot 1	Slot 2	Uniform
DuBarry	MP5SD5	.45 Mark SD	Heartbeat Sensor	Electronics Kit	Black Light

Strategy

Because you don't have to kill anybody, this mission may seem easy, but this actually makes it tougher. Your operatives must stay out of sight. If any guard spots them, the mission fails.

In addition, you can't kill any guards. You're taking weapons only because an empty slot for them isn't an option. The key to this mission is timing. You may have to play it several times to get it right—not because your strategy is flawed, but due to the difficulty of timing the guards' patrol paths.

You'll need two teams for this mission, each comprising a single electronics specialist. Any more will increase the possibility of detection. The heartbeat sensors are a must for this mission, because you must know where the enemy is without being spotted yourself. When he walks back to the north, Red Team can make a break for the front door.

Fig. 6-71. A security system in room 1-C of the garage protects the home. You must deactivate it before you can enter the house.

Blue Team

Blue Team must enter the home, deactivate the security system, and then plant the bug on the downstairs phone. At the start of the mission, advance along the north wall and halt about halfway to the house. Wait for code Alpha, and then dash toward door 3. Use the heartbeat sensor to make sure no guards are in the driveway; then enter the garage through door 3. You'll find the

Fig. 6-72. Watch out for the guard in the backyard. As he heads south, insert Blue Team into the house.

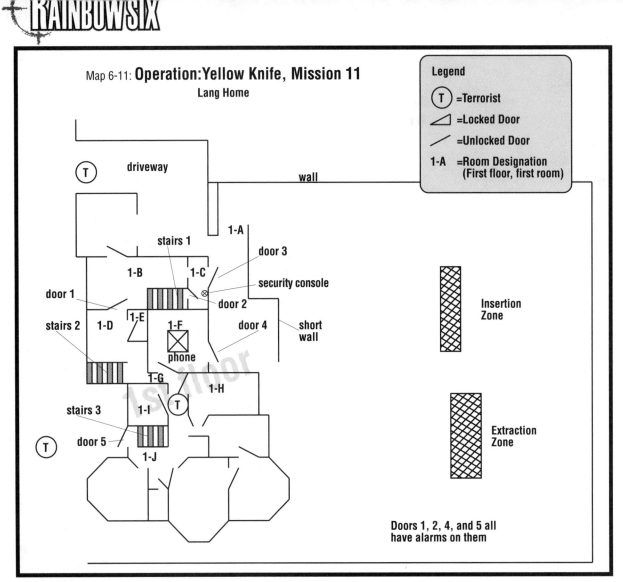

Map 6-11: Operation: Yellow Knife, Mission 11
Lang Home

Legend

(T) = Terrorist

◿ = Locked Door

╱ = Unlocked Door

1-A = Room Designation
(First floor, first room)

driveway

wall

(T)

stairs 1

1-A

door 3

1-B   1-C

security console

door 1

door 2

stairs 2   1-D   1-E   1-F

door 4   short wall

phone

Insertion Zone

1-G

1-H

stairs 3   1-I   (T)

Extraction Zone

door 5

(T)   1-J

Doors 1, 2, 4, and 5 all have alarms on them

1st floor

security keypad in 1-C. Deactivate it by approaching it and pressing 0 on the numeric keypad. Then enter the home quickly through door 1 and hide in the laundry room until you get another code Alpha.

At the next code Alpha, advance down hall 1-D and through 1-G to room 1-F. Quickly plant the bug on the telephone (press 0 on the numeric keypad), and then run back to the laundry room. Hold for code Delta; then run out through door 3 and follow the north wall back to the extraction zone.

Red Team

Red Team must plant the bug on the upstairs phone and monitor the guard on this level so Blue Team will know when it's safe to plant the bug on the other phone. Advance along the south wall

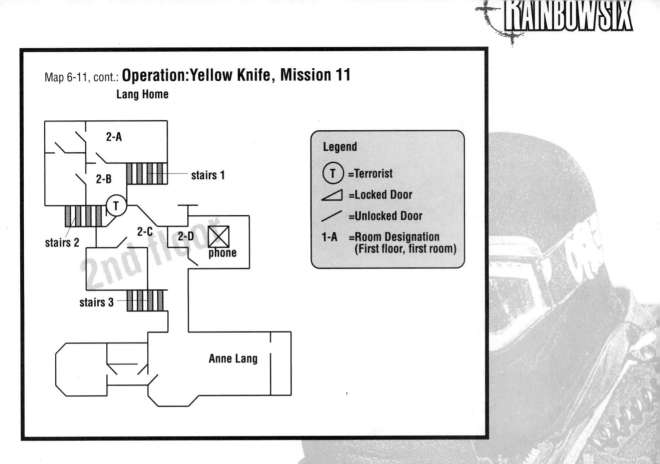

Map 6-11, cont.: **Operation:Yellow Knife, Mission 11**

Lang Home

2-A

2-B — stairs 1

T

stairs 2 2-C 2-D
phone

2nd floor

stairs 3

Anne Lang

Legend

(T) =Terrorist

◁ =Locked Door

/ =Unlocked Door

1-A =Room Designation
(First floor, first room)

and hold about halfway to the house for code Bravo. Then advance quickly around the south side of the house. When the guards on the front lawn are walking away, move to door 5 at the front of the house. Make sure the downstairs guard isn't around before entering the front door. Immediately climb stairway 3.

Pause at the top of the stairs to make sure the upstairs guard isn't looking before you run into room 2-B and plant the bug on the phone. Move into the room's alcove and monitor the upstairs guard for Blue Team and await code Bravo.

Then run to stairway 2 when the upstairs guard is walking away from you and the downstairs guard is in the south part of the house. Move into the garage. Taking care the backyard guard can't see you in the garage, hide behind a wall. Use the

Fig. 6-73. Blue Team enters the garage through door 3.

Fig. 6-74. The laundry room is a good place to hide: the downstairs guard doesn't patrol this part of the house.

Fig. 6-75. Office 1-F is a difficult room to plant a bug in. The downstairs security guard enters it regularly, and the upstairs guard checks it routinely through the opening up above.

Fig. 6-76. Red Team plants the bug on the upstairs phone. Afterward, wait in the alcove and monitor the upstairs guard for Blue Team.

heartbeat sensor to make sure there are no guards in the driveway to the north and that the backyard guard is headed south. At code Delta, which comes when the coast is clear, run along the north wall to the extraction zone.

Notes

Again, timing and stealth are the keys to this mission. You should lead Red Team, because its main job is to monitor guards and make sure the way is clear for Blue Team. At the first Bravo code waypoint (about halfway to the house), watch the backyard guard through the Sniper view of your submachine gun. Make sure the safety is on, so you don't accidentally shoot. When the guard heads south past the large window, give code Alpha. Blue Team will dash to the garage, enter, and disarm the security system.

When the guard heads back north, give code Bravo and run to the south side of the house. When the front yard is clear, go through the front door to the upstairs phone. With Red Team in the alcove and Blue in the laundry room, it's time to use those heartbeat sensors. Switch to Map view. Switching teams enables you to monitor both upstairs and downstairs guards. When the latter is in the south part of the house and the former moves south toward room 2-D, give code Alpha. Blue Team will dash into the office, plant the bug, and return to the laundry room.

The final step is getting your teams to safety. Continue monitoring the guards. When the path is clear, get Red Team downstairs and into the garage. Monitor the outside guards and give code Delta when it's safe to leave the home and head to the extraction zone.

MISSION 12—OPERATION: DEEP MAGIC

09.26.00   0400
San Francisco

Mission Orders

Horizon Corporation has been linked to the Phoenix Group. Horizon's central computer system is believed to contain information about Phoenix's plans to release the *Ebola brahma* virus.

The computer system is at Horizon's headquarters in downtown San Francisco. Access is through a terminal in John Brightling's office on the top floor. To escape detection, the team first must disable the security cameras in the control room on the floor below. Armed guards patrol both areas.

A helicopter will insert you on the roof and extract you the same way. The team must enter and leave the building completely undetected if it is to gather useful intelligence.

USE OF DEADLY FORCE IS NOT SANCTIONED ON THIS MISSION.

Fig. 6-77. If you run into Anne Lang, you not only compromise the mission, but you've taken a wrong turn somewhere.

Objective

1. Deactivate security.
2. Download files.
3. Get to extraction zone.

Fig. 6-78. Your teams must infiltrate the Horizon Corporation office building and download files from the computer database.

Mission Data

Difficulty Level	Terrorists	Hostages	Other
Recruit	3	0	6 Cameras
Veteran	3	0	6 Cameras
Elite	6	0	6 Cameras

Tom Clancy's RAINBOW SIX

Team Assignments

Blue Team

Operative	Primary	Secondary	Slot 1	Slot 2	Uniform
Lofquist	MP5SD5	.45 Mark SD	Heartbeat Sensor	Electronics Kit	Urban Light

Red Team

Operative	Primary	Secondary	Slot 1	Slot 2	Uniform
DuBarry	MP5SD5	.45 Mark SD	Heartbeat Sensor	Electronics Kit	Urban Light

Fig. 6-79. The mission will end if you move in front of these cameras before they're deactivated.

Fig. 6-80. Download the files from the database in Brightling's office on level 5.

Strategy

This mission is similar to the last. In fact, you can use the same teams in different uniforms.

Your objective is to download files from the computer database. To do this, you must get into John Brightling's office on level 5. However, security cameras cover the corridors to the office and his office door has an alarm. Therefore, you must deactivate the security system first. One team must get to the security system on level 3 and shut it down while the other gets the computer files. Then get both your teams back to the extraction zone on the roof.

Again, stealth and timing are vital to mission success. All told, only three guards patrol levels 3 and 5. Avoid them: if they spot you, the mission fails. You may not shoot them.

Blue Team

Blue Team's task is to get the files from the computer database. From where the helicopter drops you on the roof, descend stairway 1 to level 3. Hold in the stairwell until you get code Alpha, signifying the security system has been deactivated.

Use the heartbeat sensor to locate this level's two guards. Wait until they're both out near the lobby walkways in area 5-E. Exit the stairway into hall 5-A and run down halls 5-B and 5-C until you reach

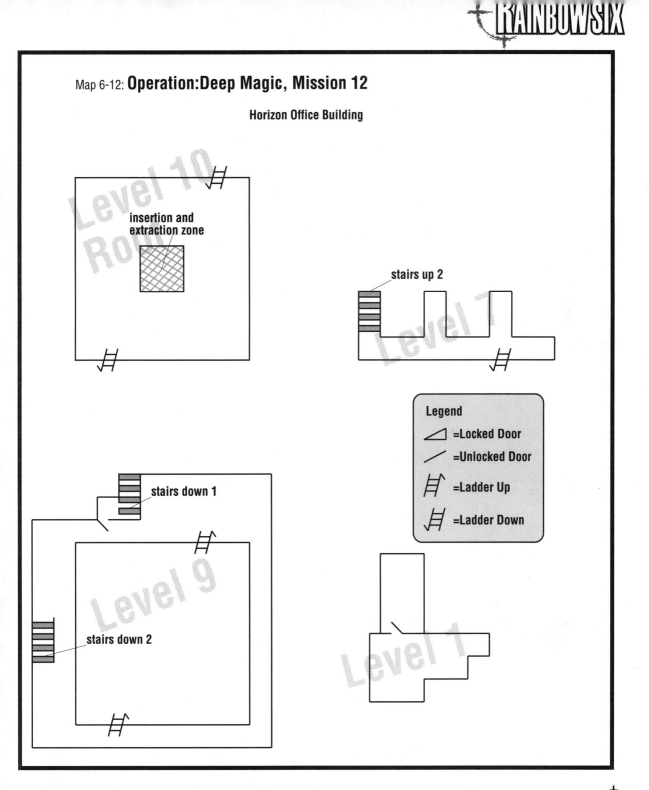

Map 6-12: **Operation:Deep Magic, Mission 12**

Horizon Office Building

Level 10
Roof

insertion and extraction zone

stairs up 2

Level 7

Legend

◿ =Locked Door

╱ =Unlocked Door

⊞ =Ladder Up

⊞ =Ladder Down

stairs down 1

Level 9

stairs down 2

Level 1

Map 6-12, cont.: **Operation:Deep Magic, Mission 12**

Horizon Office Building

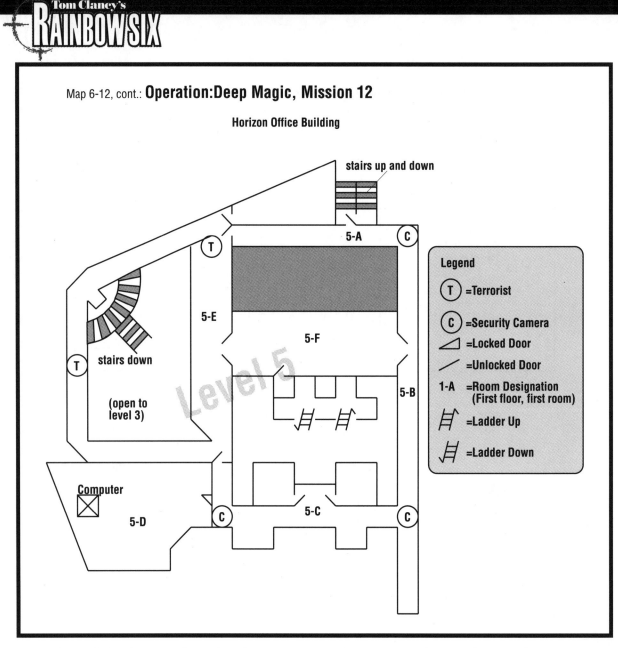

stairs up and down

5-A

5-E

5-F

5-B

T stairs down

(open to level 3)

Level 5

Computer

5-D

5-C

Legend

T =Terrorist

C =Security Camera

◁ =Locked Door

╱ =Unlocked Door

1-A =Room Designation
(First floor, first room)

=Ladder Up

=Ladder Down

5-D's door. If the doors to the right of 5-D are open, close them so the guards can't observe your actions. Pick the lock and enter the office. Walk to the computer and press ⓪ on the numeric keypad to download the files.

You have what you came for, so exit the level the way you entered, careful to avoid the guards. If you have to, you can duck into 5-F as an intermediate hiding place on your way to the stairwell. Or, if the area is clear, descend the stairs near 5-E to the lobby below and run either to the stairway or to the elevator shaft Red Team used. Return to the roof and a helicopter will pick you up and take you to safety.

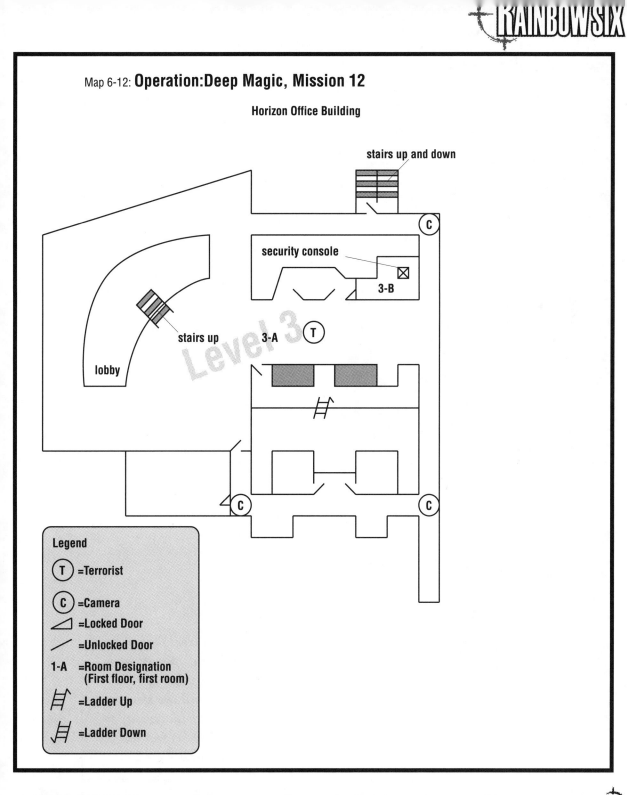

Map 6-12: **Operation:Deep Magic, Mission 12**

Horizon Office Building

stairs up and down

security console

3-B

stairs up

3-A

T

lobby

Level 3

C

C

C

Legend

T =Terrorist

C =Camera

=Locked Door

=Unlocked Door

1-A =Room Designation
(First floor, first room)

=Ladder Up

=Ladder Down

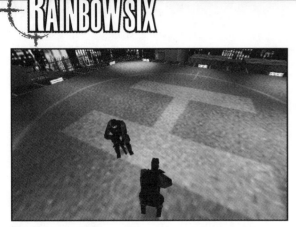

Fig. 6-81. Both teams wait on the roof for their ride out of here.

Fig. 6-82. Watch for the guard on level 3. If you can see him through the window, he can see you, too.

Fig. 6-83. Red Team must deactivate the security system before Blue Team can get the computer files.

Red Team

Red Team must deactivate the security system so Blue Team can complete its task. From the roof, descend stairway 2 to level 7. Then, in the elevator shaft, climb down two ladders to level 3. Walk to the door, but be careful: it has a window. Use the heartbeat sensor to locate this level's single guard. When he heads away from hall 3-A, give code Bravo, exit the elevator shaft access, and run to room 3-B. Pick the lock and enter.

Go to the security system and press $\boxed{0}$ on the numeric keypad to deactivate it. Now all monitors will show a loop of prerecorded feed and the door to Brightling's office is off the alarm circuit. Your job is done. Return to the roof, either the way you came or up through stairway 1.

Notes

Control Red Team during the first part of this mission. Get the team down to level 3, deactivate the security system, and then send them back to the roof for extraction. Meanwhile, Blue Team will hold for code Alpha in stairway 1 on level 5. Take control of this team. Lead it into the office to download the files and then get it back to the roof. The heartbeat sensor again proves invaluable.

Note

This level makes for a great multiplayer game. There are lots of little offices and the elevator shaft provides a way to sneak up behind the enemy undetected.

MISSION 13—OPERATION: LONE FOX

09.30.00   1900
Australia

Mission Orders

The Phoenix Group plans to release the *E. brahma* pathogen at the closing ceremonies of the Olympic Games in Sydney. Bill Hendrickson, Global Security's head of operations, has been implicated in the plot. You must take him into custody.

The team must intercept Hendrickson's motorcade. A roadblock has been set up on a deserted stretch of highway. The team must move into position before the motorcade arrives, neutralize Hendrickson's bodyguards, and move him safely up the road to the extraction zone.

Reports from spotters indicate that other vehicles containing Global Security agents follow several miles behind Hendrickson's car. These agents are in radio contact with Hendrickson and may try to prevent you from reaching the extraction zone.

RAINBOW commitments in Brazil require a second team to be dispatched before this team completes its operation. Some of this mission's team members may be unavailable for other missions in the near future. Plan accordingly.

Objective
1. Capture Hendrickson.

Tip

When choosing operatives for this mission, remember that you'll need some for missions in Brazil at the same time. Therefore, assign good leaders to each group.

Mission Data

Difficulty Level	Terrorists	Hostages	Other
Recruit	11	1	6 Vehicles
Veteran	16	1	9 Vehicles
Elite	23	1	9 Vehicles

Team Assignments

Blue Team

Operative	Primary	Secondary	Slot 1	Slot 2	Uniform
Bogart	M-16A2	.45 Mark 23	Frag Grenades	Frag Grenades	Desert Heavy
Filatov	M-16A2	.45 Mark 23	Frag Grenades	Frag Grenades	Desert Heavy

Red Team

Operative	Primary	Secondary	Slot 1	Slot 2	Uniform
Noronha	M-16A2	.45 Mark 23	Frag Grenades	Frag Grenades	Desert Heavy
Hanley	M-16A2	.45 Mark 23	Frag Grenades	Frag Grenades	Desert Heavy
Sweeney	M-16A2	.45 Mark 23	Frag Grenades	Frag Grenades	Desert Heavy

Green Team

Operative	Primary	Secondary	Slot 1	Slot 2	Uniform
Burke	M-16A2	.45 Mark 23	Frag Grenades	Frag Grenades	Desert Heavy
Rakuzanka	M-16A2	.45 Mark 23	Frag Grenades	Frag Grenades	Desert Heavy

Gold Team

Operative	Primary	Secondary	Slot 1	Slot 2	Uniform
Beckenbauer	M-16A2	.45 Mark 23	Frag Grenades	Frag Grenades	Desert Heavy

Fig. 6-84. Teams Red and Green climb the ridge overlooking the road. Make sure none of your operatives is out in the road when the motorcade arrives, or they'll be run down.

Strategy

This mission differs considerably from any mission you've been assigned in the past. All action takes place outdoors, and your teams are out in the open most of the time.

Divide your eight operatives into four teams— three fire teams and one escort team.

Much of the combat you'll experience will be at long range against tangos in body armor, so bring along the M-16s. The key to this mission is to move quickly. Once you have the hostage, move out. The enemy will send reinforcements in at three places along your path. If you can get your teams there first, you can set up an ambush. It requires careful team–waypoint coordination and Go code choices to keep your teams in positions they can support one another from.

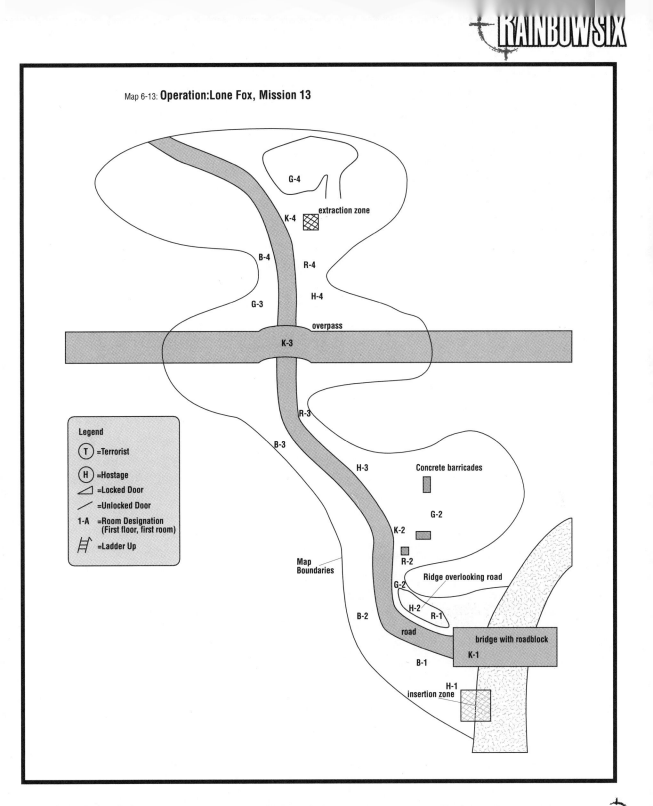

Map 6-13: **Operation:Lone Fox, Mission 13**

G-4

extraction zone

K-4

B-4

R-4

G-3

H-4

overpass

K-3

R-3

B-3

Legend

(T) =Terrorist

(H) =Hostage

◺ =Locked Door

╱ =Unlocked Door

1-A =Room Designation
(First floor, first room)

🪜 =Ladder Up

H-3

Concrete barricades

G-2

K-2

R-2

Map
Boundaries

G-2

Ridge overlooking road

H-2

R-1

B-2

road

bridge with roadblock

K-1

B-1

H-1

insertion zone

Fig. 6-85. Blue Team ambushes the motorcade from behind, while Red Team fires down on them from the ridge.

Blue Team

Blue Team must take the left side of the advance and provide fire support for Red and Green teams. At the start, move to position B-1, just off the road with a good view to the bridge where the roadblock is set up. Hold here with an Alpha code.

The motorcade will pass you and stop on the bridge at the first kill zone (K-1). Fire on the tangos as they get out, using Sniper view to aim. Take care not to hit the hostage. When all six tangos are down and you get code Alpha, advance to B-2. Wait here for code Bravo.

Another group of vehicles arrive at K-2 about a minute after the motorcade arrived at the bridge. As soon as you see them approach, switch to Sniper view and gun the tangos down as they get out. The three fire teams should have them in a cross fire. There are five tangos in this second group. When you get code Bravo, move out.

Continue down the left side of the road to B-3. This position has a good view of the overpass. Before long, two vehicles will drive up and park on the overpass at K-3. Be ready to take out the two tangos who get out to set up an ambush: you'll get them, instead.

Code Bravo orders you to move out again, this time to B-4. You're nearly to the extraction zone. Wait here for code Delta and the final wave of tango reinforcements. Two vehicles will halt at K-4 and three tangos will get out. Drop them before they realize they're too late to surprise you. After the area is clear and you get Delta, head to the extraction zone and wait for the mission to end.

Red Team

Red Team is assigned the right side of the road. At the start of the mission, move out of the river, across the road, and up the vines to the ridge overlooking the road. Take up a position at R-1 and wait for the motorcade.

Fig. 6-86. RAINBOW teams surround the tangos at the second kill zone and gun them down as they exit their vehicles.

From your location you can fire down on the tangos as they get out of their vehicles.

Once all the tangos are down and you get code Alpha, run to the next ambush position (R-2). Hide behind the concrete barricades there and await the first group of reinforcements. Gun them down as they step out of their vehicles.

The next ambush takes place at the overpass. When you get code Bravo, rush to position R-3. From there you should have a good view of the overpass and clear shots at the tangos as they get out of their vehicles. Try to find cover close to the base of the cliff the road follows.

When the overpass is clear, you'll get code Charlie. Advance to position R-4 and wait for the last group of tangos. You can conceal yourself somewhat behind the cliffside. Eliminate these tangos, and then make your way to the extraction zone at code Delta.

Green Team

Green Team is the advance team. They'll stay ahead of the other teams and try to catch the reinforcing tangos from behind. While the other teams set up the ambush for the motorcade, Green Team advances toward the next kill zone. Wait at G-1 for code Alpha; then continue to G-2. When the first group of reinforcements arrives, you can surprise them with fire in their flanks.

Fig. 6-87. Kill zone 3 on the overpass is another ambush for the enemy, if you get your teams in position in time.

After code Bravo, quickly advance to G-3, on the opposite side of the overpass. Again, you'll catch the tangos in a cross fire. When both tangos are dead and you get code Charlie, head for G-4, located on a ridge overlooking kill zone 4 (K-4). Kill the last group of tangos there, and then, at code Delta, head for the extraction zone.

Gold Team

Gold Team is tail-end Charlie. Its single operative will escort the hostage to safety. At the beginning of the mission, advance just out of the river to H-1. After the motorcade ambush, at code Alpha, go up onto the bridge and get the hostage. Escort

Fig. 6-88. Gold Team brings up the
rear, with the hostage in tow.

him to position H-2 and wait for the other teams
to take care of the tangos at K-2. At code Bravo,
move to H-3, and then H-4 at code Charlie.
When you get the all clear and code Delta, make a
beeline for the extraction zone.

Notes

As you may have concluded, you can accomplish
this mission without casualties if you ambush all
four tango groups. Timing is crucial. In fact, you
may want to keep a stopwatch handy during this mission to
make sure you stay on schedule. The following table provides
arrival times for each group of terrorists at its assigned kill
zone.

Tango Schedule

Group	Kill Zone	Time into Mission
Motorcade	Bridge (K-1)	0:45
Reinforcement 1	Construction Area (K-2)	00:01:30
Reinforcement 2	Overpass (K-3)	00:02:15
Reinforcement 3	Extraction Zone (K-4)	00:04:00

Fig. 6-89. The last group of reinforcements will stop near the extraction
zone and try to prevent your escape.

If you're up for a challenge, you can complete
this mission without encountering any reinforcements by taking out all the tangos in the motorcade in the first few seconds of the firefight. Grab
the hostage and send all your teams running for
the overpass as fast as they can. If you can get
through the construction area before the first
group of reinforcements arrives, you can reach the
extraction zone without incident.

MISSION 14—OPERATION: BLACK STAR

09.30.00   0700
Brazil

Mission Orders

The Phoenix Group has raided a research station in Brazil and taken a group of Rainforest 2000 VIPs hostage. Intelligence indicates this raid is meant to cover Anne Lang's disappearance. Surveillance reveals Lang waits with her "captors" in the main building; the other VIPs are held in a nearby prefab. The terrorists await reinforcements before killing their hostages and moving Lang out to a safe location.

Your team will be inserted by inflatable boat upriver from the station.

RAINBOW commitments in Australia require that your other team begin operations before this mission is complete.

Objective

1. Rescue all hostages.

Mission Data

Difficulty Level	Terrorists	Hostages	Other
Recruit	14	1	None
Veteran	17	3	None
Elite	20	3	None

Fig. 6-90. Anne Lang is staying in the research station with several of her tango compadres.

Team Assignments

Blue Team

Operative	Primary	Secondary	Slot 1	Slot 2	Uniform
Chavez	MP5SD5	.45 Mark SD	Flashbangs	Frag Grenades	Jungle Heavy
Yacoby	MP5SD5	.45 Mark SD	Heartbeat Sensor	Frag Grenades	Jungle Heavy

Red Team

Operative	Primary	Secondary	Slot 1	Slot 2	Uniform
Walther	MP5SD5	.45 Mark SD	Flashbangs	Frag Grenades	Jungle Heavy
Raymond	MP5SD5	.45 Mark SD	Heartbeat Sensor	Frag Grenades	Jungle Heavy

Green Team

Operative	Primary	Secondary	Slot 1	Slot 2	Uniform
Arnavisca	MP5SD5	.45 Mark SD	Flashbangs	Frag Grenades	Jungle Heavy
Maldini	MP5SD5	.45 Mark SD	Heartbeat Sensor	Frag Grenades	Jungle Heavy

Gold Team

Operative	Primary	Secondary	Slot 1	Slot 2	Uniform
Haider	MP5SD5	.45 Mark SD	Flashbangs	Frag Grenades	Jungle Heavy
Woo	MP5SD5	.45 Mark SD	Heartbeat Sensor	Frag Grenades	Jungle Heavy

Fig. 6-91. The tangos hold the VIPs in the crew barracks. You must get to them before the terrorists execute them.

Strategy

This is a stealth mission. You must keep quiet and use silenced weapons, at least until you've secured the two VIP hostages. If their tango guards hear gunshots, they may execute them.

You need four teams—two for each building. The VIPs are in the crew barracks; Anne Lang is in the research building. Securing the first building is the priority.

Although the buildings are small and contain few rooms, it's still a good idea to bring along heartbeat sensors to see what's in a room before you enter. Coordination is essential in entering the buildings. You'll have a better chance for success if two teams rush in at the same time from different

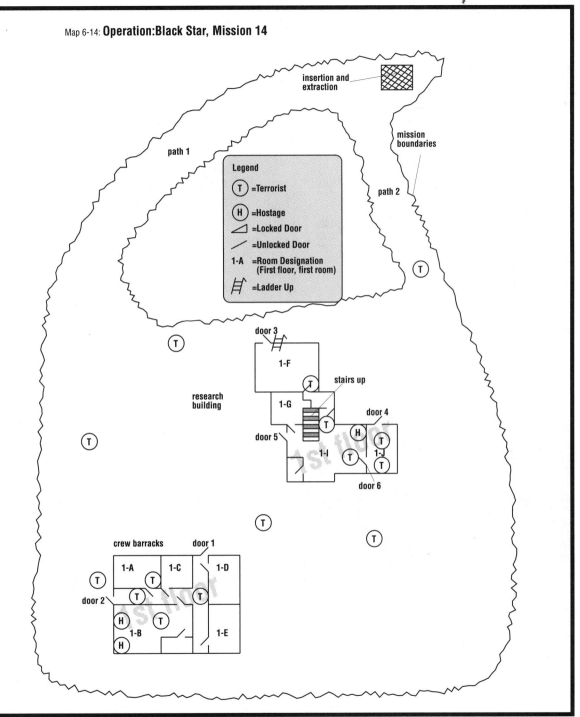

Map 6-14: **Operation:Black Star, Mission 14**

insertion and extraction

mission boundaries

path 1

path 2

Legend

(T) =Terrorist

(H) =Hostage

◿ =Locked Door

╱ =Unlocked Door

1-A =Room Designation
(First floor, first room)

▦ =Ladder Up

door 3

1-F

stairs up

(T)

research building

1-G

door 4

door 5

(H) (T)

1-I 1-J

(T) (T) (T)

(T) (T)

door 6

(T)

(T)

(T)

crew barracks   door 1

1-A   1-C   1-D

(T) (T) (T)

door 2   (T)   1st floor

(H) (T)

1-B   1-E

(H)

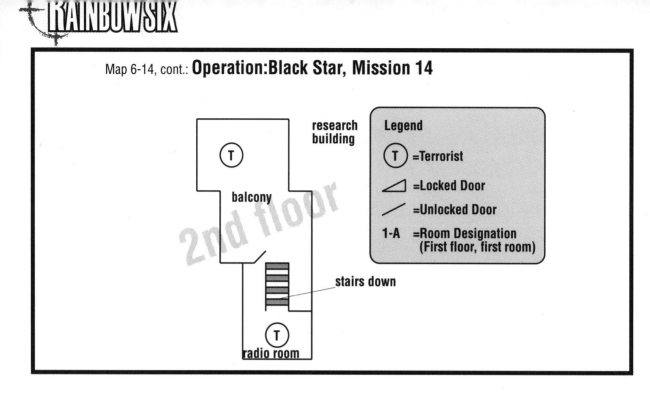

Map 6-14, cont.: **Operation:Black Star, Mission 14**

research
building

balcony

2nd floor

Legend

(T) =Terrorist

◿ =Locked Door

╱ =Unlocked Door

1-A =Room Designation
(First floor, first room)

stairs down

radio room

entrances. (Be careful of blue-on-blue, or friendly fire.) After you rescue the hostages, get them back to the extraction zone.

Fig. 6-92. Blue Team can open up most of the clearing with long-range fire using Sniper view from the end of the jungle path.

Blue Team

Blue Team is the advance group for the other teams. Climb the rope ladder and take path 1 toward the station. Hold for code Alpha at the clearing entrance. However, while you're here, switch to Sniper view and take out the three tangos near the crew quarters. You must kill all three quickly. Survivors will run inside and kill the hostages. If you move into the clearing a bit, you also can take out the tango on the balcony of the research building. Scan the rest of the area for other tangos on patrol.

At code Alpha, run to the crew quarters and wait by door 2 for code Charlie. Then rush in with Green Team and clear out the building. The hostages are in room 1-B. A tango may be with them. There's another tango in 1-A and possibly one in 1-E.

When the hostages are secure, exit the quarters and make a quick patrol around the building. Then lead Green Team and the hostages to safety at code Delta, following the route you took into the station clearing.

Red Team

Red Team must clear the research building. Follow path 2 to the clearing. You may find a tango along the way. Take him down before he can sound an alarm. Hold just short of the clearing and wait for Alpha. Then make your way to the ladder outside room 1-F. Climb it to the balcony and enter the door to the radio room. A tango hides in the corner. Sidestep around the corner and drop him with a burst of gunfire.

Carefully descend the stairs to room 1-G. There may be a tango in room 1-H. Take him out if he's there. Hold in room 1-G for code Bravo. When the code comes, rush into 1-I, along with Gold Team, and take out the two tangos there. Take care not to shoot Anne Lang. Wait for code Delta, and then lead Gold Team and Lang back to the extraction zone.

Green Team

Green Team provides support to Blue Team. Take path 1 to the clearing and hold for Alpha. At the code, run to door 1 of the crew barracks and wait for Charlie. This is the go for rushing into the building along with Blue Team. Take out tangos in 1-E and 1-B to secure the hostages. When you're ready to escort them, wait for code Delta to begin leading them back down path 1 to the extraction zone.

Gold Team

Gold Team provides support for Red Team. Follow path 2 to the clearing and hold for Alpha. Then rush toward the green house, room 1-J, attached to the research building and take out the two tangos there, as well as any others you see outside the

Fig. 6-93. A tango unloads on Red Team: they were careless as they moved around a corner.

Fig. 6-94. Green Team rescues the two VIPs and escorts them to safety.

Fig. 6-95. Gold Team rushes into the research building with guns blazing.

Fig. 6-96. RAINBOW escorts Anne Lang to the safety of a prison cell.

buildings. Wait at door 6 for code Bravo; then rush into room 1-I to clear it and capture Anne Lang. Prepare to escort her down path 2 to the extraction zone at code Delta.

Notes

Controlling Blue Team lets you take care of things from long range at the edge of the clearing using Sniper view. After you eliminate the tangos outside the two buildings, the rest of the mission isn't that difficult, but beware of a couple of tangos who seem to appear out of nowhere. Just when you think everything is safe and you let your guard down, they show up to blow away a team or two.

It's important to coordinate your actions. Code Alpha sends all teams to their positions outside the buildings; Bravo sends Red and Gold into room 1-I; Charlie orders Blue and Green to rush the crew barracks. Try giving both orders at once. Red and Gold can handle their tasks under computer control. When all hostages are secure, give code Delta to send the four teams back down the jungle paths to the extraction zone.

MISSION 15—OPERATION: WILD ARROW

10.01.00   0300
Sydney

Mission Orders

Phoenix has planted virus bombs in the air circulation system of the athlete's village in Sydney. They're timed to go off just before the closing ceremonies of the Olympic Games.

The bombs are tied together through the village's computerized climate control system. Disarming them is a two-stage process: You must shut off the central computer first, and then disable both bombs individually inside a 30-second window. If you miss this window of opportunity, or tamper with the bombs before the computer is shut down, they'll release their lethal contents.

Phoenix Group members dressed as Global Security guards patrol the area. Alarm panels are scattered throughout the village underground. If the team's presence is detected and the alarm is raised, the terrorists will release the virus manually. You may use deadly force against the guards if you must.

Your team will be inserted into the sewers below the village.

Fig. 6-97. The virus capsules have been placed in the air system's heating and cooling ducts. Once they're activated, the virus will spread through the entire building within minutes.

Objective

1. Disable both virus capsules.

Mission Data

Difficulty Level	Terrorists	Hostages	Other
Recruit	13	5	1 Capsule
Veteran	16	5	2 Capsules
Elite	16	5	3 Capsules

Team Assignments

Blue Team

Operative	Primary	Secondary	Slot 1	Slot 2	Uniform
Bogart	MP5SD5	.45 Mark SD	Primary Mag	Empty	Urban Medium
DuBarry	MP5SD5	.45 Mark SD	Heartbeat Sensor	Electronics Kit	Urban Medium

Red Team

Operative	Primary	Secondary	Slot 1	Slot 2	Uniform
Noronha	MP5SD5	.45 Mark SD	Primary Mag	Empty	Urban Medium
Beckenbauer	MP5SD5	.45 Mark SD	Heartbeat Sensor	Demolitions Kit	Urban Medium

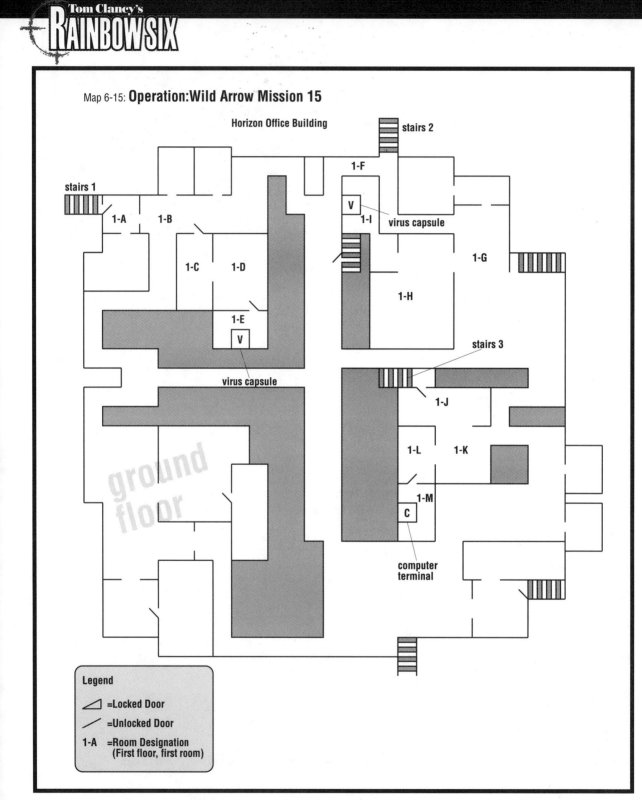

Map 6-15: **Operation:Wild Arrow Mission 15**

Horizon Office Building

stairs 2

1-F

stairs 1

1-A

1-B

V

1-I

virus capsule

1-C

1-D

1-G

1-H

1-E

V

virus capsule

stairs 3

1-J

ground floor

1-L

1-K

1-M

C

computer terminal

Legend

◿ =Locked Door

╱ =Unlocked Door

1-A =Room Designation
(First floor, first room)

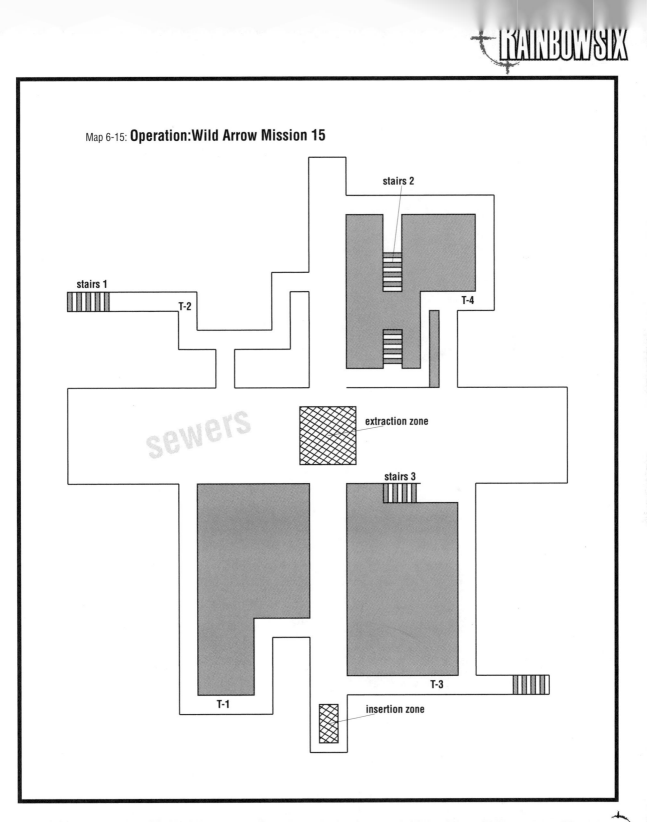

Map 6-15: **Operation:Wild Arrow Mission 15**

stairs 2

stairs 1

T-2

T-4

sewers

extraction zone

stairs 3

T-1

T-3

insertion zone

Green Team

Operative	Primary	Secondary	Slot 1	Slot 2	Uniform
Hanley	MP5SD5	.45 Mark SD	Primary Mag	Empty	Urban Medium
Morris	MP5SD5	.45 Mark SD	Heartbeat Sensor	Demolitions Kit	Urban Medium

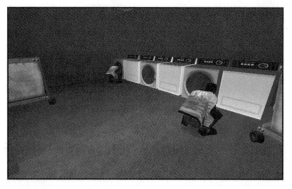

Fig. 6-98. There are five civilians in the building. Try not to get them killed in a cross fire between your teams and the tangos.

Strategy

This mission isn't as hard as some of the previous ones, but it includes a variable that can make planning difficult: Most of the guards are on patrol paths. This means you must plan for opposition throughout most of the mission. One group of three tangos patrols the entire ground floor in a circuit. If one of your teams runs into them, it could be messy. There are a number of alarm boxes throughout the ground floor. If a tango spots one of your teams, you must kill him before he can sound the alarm. The alarm will cause the premature release of the viruses and end the mission in failure for you—and for the world.

There are five civilians in the building, as well, but they're all crouched down. Take care stray fire doesn't hit them.

Timing is of utmost importance. You must deactivate the triggering device for the virus capsules at the computer terminal, and then disarm both capsules within 30 seconds. To accomplish this, you'll need three teams. The team deactivating the computer trigger should include an electronics expert and the other two demolitions specialists. Your teams begin in the sewer tunnels beneath the athletic village. From there, they must gain access to the ground floor, locate the various devices, and deactivate them within the time limits.

Fig. 6-99. Be careful as you advance to the virus capsules. Tangos patrol the entire ground level.

Blue Team

Blue Team's job is to deactivate the computer trigger device. From the insertion zone, head down tunnel 3 to stairway 3. Go up the stairs and hold at the door for Alpha. Use the heartbeat sensor to locate tangos in the area. When it looks clear, make

your way quickly, but cautiously, through room
1-J, to 1-K, 1-L, and finally 1-M. Take out any tangos you encounter on the way, but do it silently.

The computer terminal is in room 1-H. Wait
for code Bravo, and then deactivate the triggering
device. The rest of the mission is up to the other
two teams. Cross your fingers and hope they can
disarm the capsules within 30 seconds.

Red Team

Red Team is one of the capsule-disarming teams.
From the insertion zone, advance down tunnel 1 to
the main sewer tunnel. Two tangos patrol this area.
Take out the one closest to you—and the other, if
another team hasn't shot him already.

Continue through tunnel 2 to stairway 1.
Ascend to the ground level, but hold for code
Alpha before opening the door from the stairway.
At Alpha, move into room 1-A and on through 1-
B and 1-C to room 1-D, where the first virus cap-
sule lies. Wait for Blue Team to deactivate the trig-
gering device before touching the capsule. Code
Charlie tells you it's safe to begin disarming it.
Work quickly, because the capsule will release the
virus on its own 30 seconds after the trigger is
deactivated.

Green Team

Green Team must get to the *other* virus capsule
and disarm it. From the insertion zone, move
down tunnel 3 to the main sewer area. Take out
the tangos patrolling there, and then continue to
stairway 2 via tunnel 4. Climb the stairs and wait
at the door for code Alpha. Use caution as you
enter hall 1-F and go through 1-G and 1-H to
room 1-I. Wait for Charlie before disarming the
capsule. You have 30 seconds to do so.

Fig. 6-100. You must deactivate the
triggering device at the computer terminal before you can disarm the virus
capsules.

Fig. 6-101. There are two tangos down
in the main sewer. Take them out
using Sniper view.

Fig. 6-102. The computer terminal
and virus capsules are located in the
ventilation rooms.

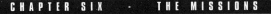

Notes

You should control Blue Team: its task must be completed first. All teams enter the first floor at code Alpha. When all are at their assigned tasks, code Bravo instructs Blue Team to deactivate the computer triggering device. When it has, immediately give code Charlie, so Red and Green Teams can begin disarming the virus capsules. After both are neutralized, the mission ends a success.

The patrolling guards make this mission difficult, especially for computer-controlled teams, which don't always use the heartbeat sensor to their benefit. Consider controlling all teams. Have each hold at the stairway doors to the ground floor. Then lead each to its destination to wait for you to position the other teams. Then give Bravo and Charlie codes to disable the doomsday devices.

Fig. 6-103. Take care when you move through the large rooms. Tangos can pop up anywhere. Use the heartbeat sensor to prevent them from ambushing you.

MISSION 16—OPERATION: MYSTIC TIGER

10.01.00   0600
Brazil

Fig. 6-104. Capture John Brightling and bring him to justice.

Mission Orders

John Brightling and the remnants of the Phoenix/Horizon conspiracy have barricaded themselves in the Horizon "Ark." The Ark consists of three habitat domes and an inner survival bunker, where Brightling is believed to be hiding. Brazilian troops surround the compound, but RAINBOW has been asked to lead the assault.

Some of the Ark's occupants may be willing to surrender peacefully. Avoid unnecessary bloodshed, but keep in mind that the safety of the team and the capture of John Brightling have priority.

Because the tangos may have released the *E. brahma* virus within the Ark, biosuits are highly recommended.

Objective

1. Capture Brightling.

Mission Data

Difficulty Level	Terrorists	Hostages	Other
Recruit	29	15	Brightling
Veteran	29	15	Brightling
Elite	29	15	Brightling

Team Assignments

Blue Team

Operative	Primary	Secondary	Slot 1	Slot 2	Uniform
Chavez	CAR-15	.45 Mark 23	Frag Grenades	Flashbangs	Biosuit
Yacoby	CAR-15	.45 Mark 23	Frag Grenades	Heartbeat Sensor	Biosuit

Red Team

Operative	Primary	Secondary	Slot 1	Slot 2	Uniform
Walther	CAR-15	.45 Mark-23	Frag Grenades	Flashbangs	Biosuit
Arnavisca	CAR-15	.45 Mark-23	Frag Grenades	Flashbangs	Biosuit
Raymond	CAR-15	.45 Mark-23	Frag Grenades	Heartbeat Sensor	Biosuit

Green Team

Operative	Primary	Secondary	Slot 1	Slot 2	Uniform
Bogart	CAR-15	.45 Mark 23	Frag Grenades	Flashbangs	Biosuit
Rakuzanka	CAR-15	.45 Mark 23	Frag Grenades	Flashbangs	Biosuit
Maldini	CAR-15	.45 Mark 23	Frag Grenades	Heartbeat Sensor	Biosuit

Strategy

This mission makes the previous missions look like boot camp. It's extremely difficult: the enemy has set up areas to ambush your teams as they advance through the Ark. Because there are three insertion zones, you may be tempted to split your force into three groups. But you can't split up your force and expect to make it to area 4 with even half of your operatives alive.

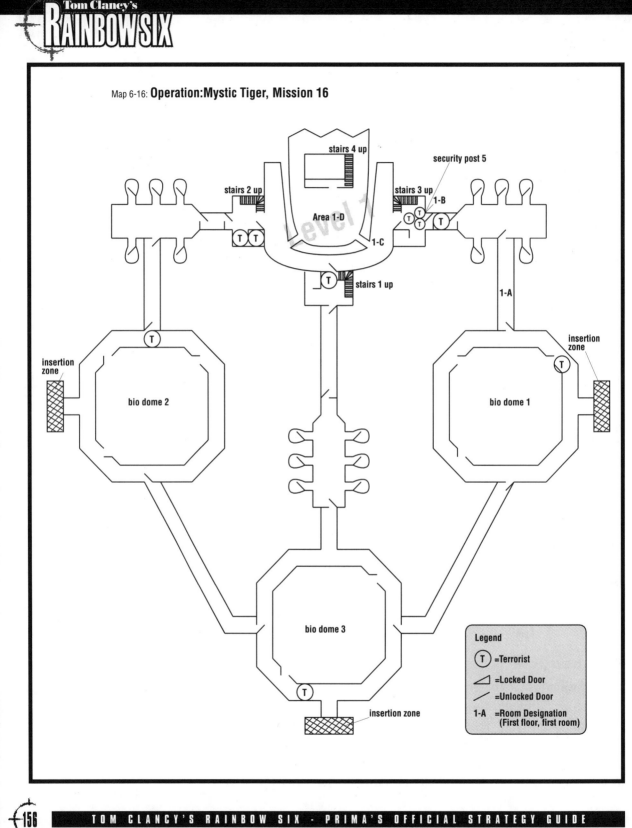

Map 6-16: **Operation:Mystic Tiger, Mission 16**

stairs 4 up

security post 5

stairs 2 up

stairs 3 up

1-B

Area 1-D

1-C

1-A

stairs 1 up

insertion zone

insertion zone

bio dome 2

bio dome 1

insertion zone

bio dome 3

insertion zone

Legend

(T) =Terrorist

=Locked Door

=Unlocked Door

1-A =Room Designation
(First floor, first room)

Map 6-16, cont.: Operation:Mystic Tiger, Mission 16

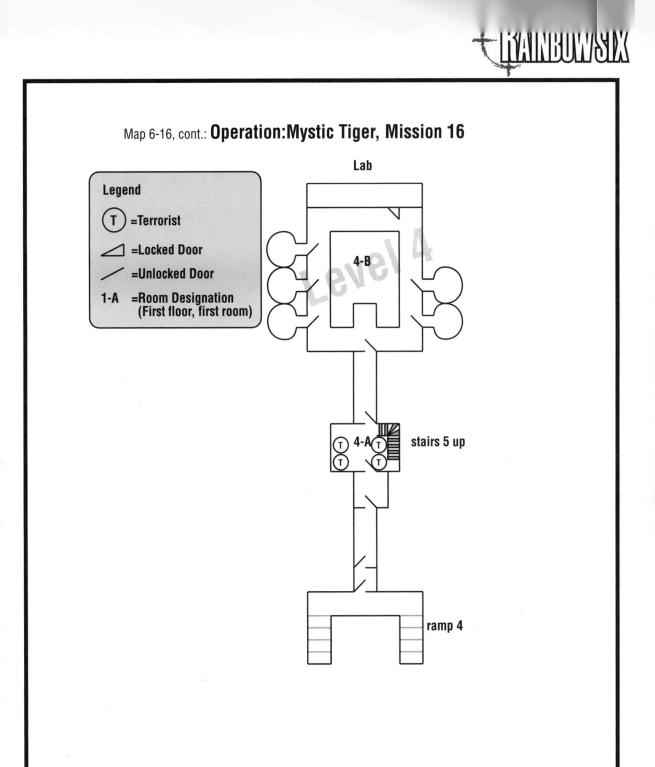

Lab

Legend

(T) = Terrorist

◁ = Locked Door

╱ = Unlocked Door

1-A = Room Designation
(First floor, first room)

Level 4

4-B

4-A

stairs 5 up

ramp 4

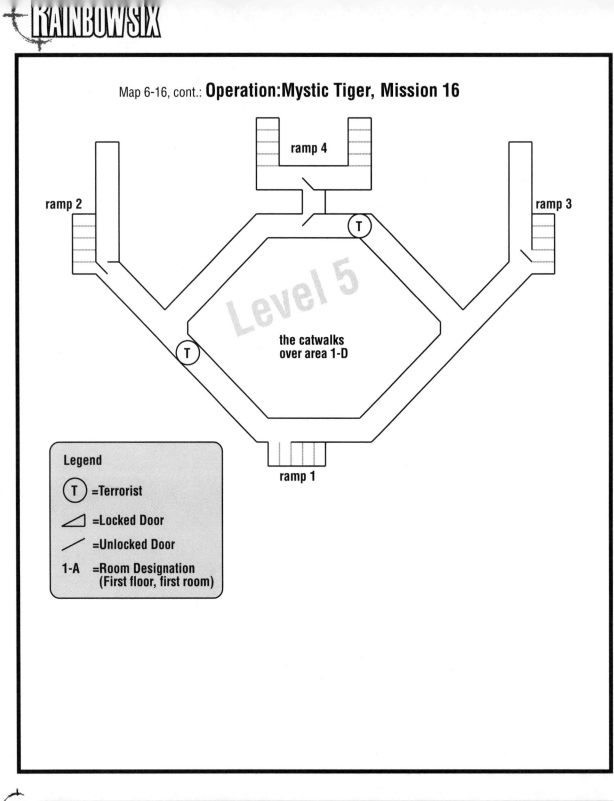

Map 6-16, cont.: **Operation:Mystic Tiger, Mission 16**

ramp 4

ramp 2

ramp 3

Level 5

the catwalks
over area 1-D

ramp 1

Legend

(T) =Terrorist

◺ =Locked Door

╱ =Unlocked Door

1-A =Room Designation
(First floor, first room)

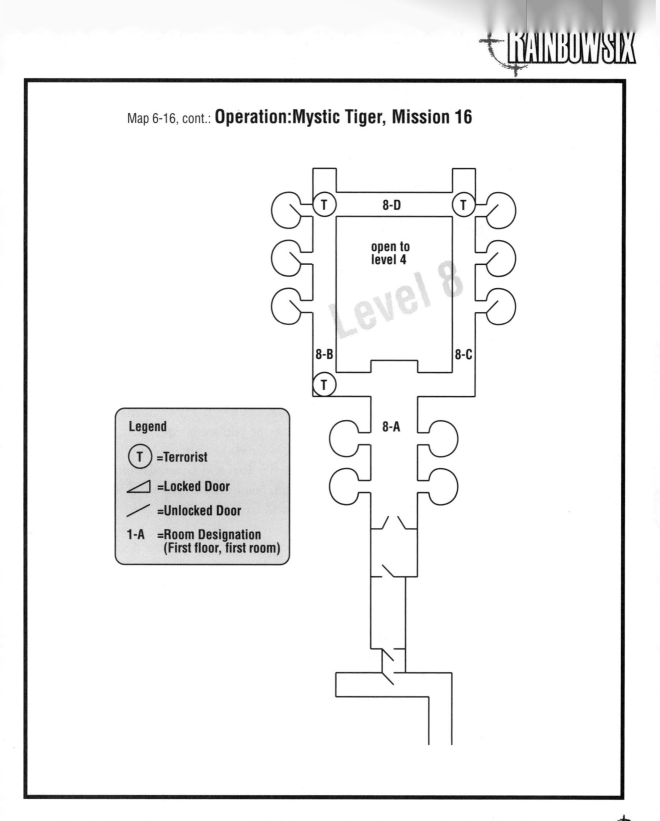

Map 6-16, cont.: **Operation:Mystic Tiger, Mission 16**

8-D

open to
level 4

Level 8

8-B   8-C

8-A

Legend

(T) =Terrorist

=Locked Door

=Unlocked Door

1-A =Room Designation
(First floor, first room)

Fig. 6-105. Insert your three teams into biodome 1.

Fig. 6-106. All three teams get ready to rush security post 1-B.

Fig. 6-107. Blue Team takes out the tangos on the catwalks from area 1-D, below.

Instead, organize your eight operatives into three teams, but keep the teams together. This may make it hard to get through some narrow doorways; you need all the firepower you can get to make it through to Brightling. All teams will use the same strategy.

Insert all teams into biodome 1. From there, make your way toward stairway 3 and security post 1-B. You'll encounter a few tangos along the way. Halt all teams in the corridor before you reach security post 1-B and wait for code Alpha. Position Green team in the middle of the corridor, Red on the right, and Blue, the team you control, on the left.

Inch Blue Team carefully along the left wall. Use the heartbeat sensor to locate the tangos inside. There will be three to five, with one on the stairs above. When the door opens automatically, shoot anyone you see inside. Then throw a frag grenade around the corner as you give code Alpha, which sends Red and Green dashing in to clear the room. Send the two teams up the stairs to level 5 and have them hold outside the door to the catwalks over area 1-D.

Now take Blue Team to the doorway into this large open area. You may run into a tango or two down this corridor. At the doorway, slowly side-step around the corner to get a view of the catwalks. Use Sniper view and take out the two tangos patrolling up there. If you get only one, send the other teams rushing out onto the catwalks with code Bravo. Then join them on the catwalk by ascending stairway 3. Move all teams across the catwalks to ramp 4, in the silver building.

Head up the ramp to level 8. Advance to room 8-A, and then split Red and Green teams. Send Red down to hold at 8-B while Green waits at 8-C. Code Charlie sends them both into room 8-D to take out the two or three tangos on the walkways above level 4. Get all your teams back to ramp 4 and then down to level 4.

Room 4-A is a security post—and a death trap. It's configured like the post you stormed on level 1. Position Blue on the left, Green in the center, and Red on the right. Use the heartbeat sensor to take a look at what you face, and then inch forward until the door opens. At code Delta, Red and Green rush in and kill everyone who remains alive in the room.

These are the last tangos you'll have to kill in this campaign. All that remains is to capture John Brightling. Enter the lab and pick the lock to the big metal door to end the mission and the campaign.

Good job!

Notes

Expect to lose some operatives no matter how carefully you plan and execute this mission. It's a dangerous one, and the biosuits, while protective against deadly viruses, do little to stop a bullet. Also, the automatic doors make surprising the enemy difficult. When setting waypoints with Go codes, take care not to place a waiting team so close to a door that it opens prematurely. Before entering any security post, use the heartbeat sensor to see where tangos are positioned. The sensor can't "see" tangos on the landing above a post, and each post has at least one tango up on these landings.

This mission tests your tactics, as the foregoing strategy shows. Once you complete it, pat yourself on the back. You just saved all of humankind.

Fig. 6-108. Ramp 4 is inside the silver building in the middle of area 1-D.

Fig. 6-109. Red and Green blitz area 8-D to secure the area above the lab on level 4.

Fig. 6-110. You face this mission's (and the campaign's) last opposition at security post 4-A. Beyond this, it's a clean walk to John Brightling in the lab.

Rainbow Six's multiplayer function makes for some remarkable gameplay. One terrific feature is its speech capability. The game is so fast-paced, you could be killed in the time it takes to type a message or to taunt another player. But with an inexpensive microphone plugged into a sound card or other device, players can speak directly to one another. A headset works best, but a clip-on mike with speakers works almost as well.

There are two ways to play *Rainbow Six* with other humans—cooperate in one of the game's 16 missions, or fight against each other on any of the game maps. You can connect to play over a Local Area Network, on the Internet, or using Mplayer. Follow the game manual's directions, or those of your service provider, if you have trouble connecting.

From the Multiplayer screen, you may choose either to host a game or to join one another player has created. The host chooses mission type, location, and other game specifics. Players may choose their own characters and the weapons and equipment they'll carry.

The following sections provide details on the types of games you can play in multiplayer *Rainbow Six*.

COOPERATIVE MISSIONS

In cooperative multiplayer, as you might expect, players work together to complete one of the campaign game's 16 missions. You can use the training facilities to hone your skills and learn to work as a team. I suggest going through the Kill Houses together before embarking on any mission.

The host may select from several options, including difficulty level and whether a player works singly or with team support. Players may choose to be any of the 20 RAINBOW operatives, but there can be only one of each personality. A chat window on the Game Creation screen facilitates mission planning. Use it to ensure team operatives carry appropriate equipment. When everyone's ready, the host can start the mission. Players begin at one of the insertion zones.

Fig. 7-1. The Game Creation Screen

COMMUNICATIONS

Communication is the single most important factor for completing any cooperative mission.

Before beginning, choose an overall leader. If there are several players, organize the operatives into teams, with leaders for each. Assign each team one or more tasks and orders for executing them. For example, if Team Blue is going to enter a house through the front door, it may have to wait until after another team disables a security system. Teams should practice in the Kill Houses and training ranges until their members are comfortable working together.

Players should study the mission maps (from the single-player mission-planning phase) ahead of time. Real antiterrorist teams learn as much as they can about a target location before they enter it. Your missions will offer enough surprises your without your getting lost. Multiplayer missions have no waypoints, so you may want to pencil some in on a hand-drawn map, or on the maps in this book.

Fig. 7-2. Team support checks the room on the other side of the door with a heartbeat sensor before the lead opens the door and enters.

TIP

The voice option adds a lot to multiplayer games. After connecting a microphone and activating speech from the multiplayer options, you can speak to your teammates or adversaries. It works like a one-channel radio: Hold down the spacebar to record your message. Release it to transmit. This is a lot easier than typing during a mission, when every second counts.

Radio Discipline

No one wants to waste a lot of mission time typing long lists of instructions for each fellow player. Even spoken messages can be confusing and easily misunderstood when they're too long. Maintaining strict radio discipline is vital.

Each message should follow a basic format. First, address the recipient; then identify yourself. Briefly state your message and end with "Over." This last word tells the receiver that you've completed your message and he or she hasn't missed any of it. Stating who the message is for and who it's from prevents confusion when you're playing with several others.

Each player should have his or her own designation. Following RAINBOW's example, the overall leader is called "Six." Other operatives can be named after team, task, and the like. For example, you could call the leader of Blue Team "Blue One." I prefer naming operatives for their tasks. An assault team might include Rifle 1 and Rifle 2, and a demolitions specialist, Demo 5, for example.

The shorter and more concise the message, the better. Recipients should respond with "Roger" or "Acknowledged," if they agree, or "Negative," if they can't comply.

Here's an example of proper radio discipline:

> *"Recon 1, Six. Status. Over."*
> *"Six, Recon 1. Tangos by front door and on balcony. Over."*
> *"Roger Recon 1. Demo 4, Six. Frag front door. Rifle 1 and Rifle 2, clear entry. Over."*
> *"Recon 1, Acknowledged."*
> *"Rifle 1, Acknowledged."*
> *"Rifle 2, Acknowledged."*
> *(Six) "Go!"*
> *(Rifle 1) "Contact!"*
> *(Rifle 2) "Got him!"*
> *(Rifle 1) "Clear."*
> *(Rifle 2) "Clear."*
> *"Rifle 1, Six. Status. Over."*
> *"Six, Rifle 1. One tango down. Escorting precious cargo. Over."*
> *(Six) "Acknowledged."*

In this example, each message was brief and to the point, but provided enough information to do the job. Notice the importance of status reports. They let other players know what's happened so the leader can order the next step.

It may take practice to become familiar with this discipline, but it makes the game far more realistic—and using it can make the difference between success and failure, especially in fast-paced missions.

Fig. 7-3. One player opens the door and covers the opening as the other lobs in a frag grenade.

Tactics

You may have developed some great single-player tactics, but multiplayer games demand a few new ones. Teamwork is among the most important. If you have enough players, group them in pairs. Two people see twice as much and can accomplish different tasks, making the team more effective.

My favorite such tactic involves using the heartbeat sensor: the leader carries a weapon while the second team member uses the heartbeat sensor to locate enemies. Everything the sensor picks up is relayed to all team members, so it becomes unnecessary for each to use his or her own.

A two-person team also is useful for breaching a door or clearing a room. One opens the door as the other tosses a frag grenade or flashbang. Both then run through the doorway and spread out, one going left and the other right. This prevents anyone getting shot in the back because he or she looked left when the tango was right. (Practice at the training ranges will help two-person teams develop the good timing such tactics require.) A second player also can help prevent surprises from the rear.

Spacing between team members also is something to think about. You want to stay close enough to support one another, but not so close that a single automatic burst could take you both out. Outdoors, you can space team members far enough apart that they can support one another without a single grenade killing both.

TIP

Each team should have at least one heartbeat sensor. Only one team member must use it, and all players on that team can see what the sensor detects.

Strategy

The single-player campaign strategies in Chapter 6 apply as well to cooperative missions.

Surviving Frag Attacks

Your enemies won't use frag grenades in the single-player campaign, but you can expect a human opponent to rely on such tactics.

Keeping your formations loose is crucial during team adversarial games. Close formations may have value in terms of mutual assistance, they also make a team a juicy target for machine-gun fire and frag grenades. Stay loose during advances and when entering new territory.

Plan for grenade attacks when defending. Never position too many of your people in a confined area. Keep your forces far from doors and other openings.

An assaulting force is likely to toss grenades in along the same wall as the door they just breached, so a position in the center of the room can be safer than one in a corner. Hiding behind furniture or other objects will increase your chance for surviving a frag attack.

ADVERSARIAL GAMES

Working together can be rewarding, but sometimes we all want to test our skills against another human. Not to worry. *Rainbow Six* includes an extensive system for doing just that. The host player can choose Kill Houses and single-player mission maps. If you thought these were challenging against the computer, wait until you try them against a human player!

The host chooses not only the mission map, but also mission type. *Rainbow Six* allows you to play more than just "last man standing." Team games are a big part of adversarial games, and you have six mission types to choose from.

Survival

Survival is the standard multiplayer game. It's every-player-for-him- or herself, and the last survivor wins. Once you're dead, you're out of the game until there's a winner. There's no resurrecting and coming back to fight in the same round.

Team Survival

Team Survival is similar to the foregoing, but you need only kill all the players on the other team.

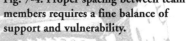
Stronghold

In Stronghold, one team defends an area while the other attacks and tries to reach and clear a certain location. Because the defender usually has the advantage, it's usually a good idea to give the attacking team more people.

Double Stronghold

Double Stronghold requires each team to defend its base while trying to capture that of the other team. This is a good choice for games with lots of players.

Double Bluff

Double Bluff gives each side a single hostage. The object is to bring the other team's hostage to your base while protecting your own hostage. Take care around the hostages, though: whoever kills one loses automatically.

Recon/Regroup

Recon/Regroup differs from the other mission types. You need achieve only one of your two objectives to complete the game. First, your team must either spot visually or kill all enemy team members. Second, you must get most of your team members back to base. Stealth is the key to either objective. Usually you should wear light uniforms and carry silenced weapons. This game type is best played on large maps with lots of players. It's similar to hide-and-seek, but both teams hide and seek at the same time.

Special Tactics

Adversarial missions, especially Survival games, demand some new and different tactics, most relating to the fact that you're operating as a single-person team, without support.

Take care when you use the heartbeat sensor. It tells you where the enemies are, but things can happen very fast. Don't get caught trying to shoot an enemy with the sensor. Take

Fig. 7-4. Proper spacing between team members requires a fine balance of support and vulnerability.

Fig. 7-5. Using team tactics, a pair of players prepares to breach a door with a shotgun. The player with the shotgun had better stay close to his partner or he'll be dead shortly. He'd be better off switching to his pistol.

Fig. 7-6. Heartbeat sensors are virtually useless on stairways. Don't let another player sneak up on you from a different level while you're concentrating on the map.

TIP

Heartbeat sensors are great for multiplayer missions, but be careful when you use them, especially in Survival games. While your sensor is active, your weapons aren't. I've killed other players who saw me on their sensors, but who couldn't then select and aim their gun before I ran around the corner and shot them dead.

quick looks and then switch back to a weapon. Use extreme caution near stairways. Because the heartbeat sensor shows other players only on your level, it's easy to be surprised by someone coming up or down the stairs.

In other multiplayer games, some players like to wait in ambush for their enemies. This is called "camping." Campers usually are unpopular and, once identified, often become targets for all the other players. Although *Rainbow Six*'s maps and levels provide lots of hiding places, the heartbeat sensor eliminates the element of surprise. In fact, while you wait for someone to come through a doorway so you can blow them away, the enemy's sensor may already have pointed you out, and you'll get a frag grenade, instead. This makes multiplayer *Rainbow Six* move more quickly than other games.

The Maps

You may choose from 17 maps in adversarial games. Each requires special consideration.

Kill House Two-Story

This is a small level, great for quick, tense, games. It's too small to be much good for anything but Stronghold games, however. The defender must deal with an assault that can come from two directions at once.

Embassy

The Embassy map works well for all game types. The three levels, with their numerous stairways and small rooms, make for great close combat. Bring along some grenades.

Congo Mansion

Again, because the mansion house is small, this map works best for Stronghold games. However, it's useful for Team Survival, as well. The large areas of open ground make it a poor choice for other game types.

Oil Rig

With its many levels, stairways, and ladders, the Oil Rig map works for any type of game.

Hacienda

This map resembles Congo Mansion, in multiplayer terms. Use it for Stronghold games. Pick off as many enemies as you can out in the open before fighting room-to-room.

Fig. 7-7. Use caution in these missions. When you die, you stay dead for the rest of the round.

Water Ride

You must try this map. Its three levels and colorful scenery make for fun games of any type. The catwalks above the large open areas make it challenging, as well.

Dam

The Dam combines narrow tunnels with large, open rooms—useful for all game types. Use care in the turbine rooms, where other players can shoot at you from different levels. Your heartbeat sensor can detect only those on your own level.

Bio Lab

Most game types can use the Bio Lab map, but the open space between the buildings can become a kill zone as enemies fire out the building windows. Also, the lab makes for claustrophobic combat and the automatic doors make surprise breaches difficult.

Airport

The Airport map has lots of open space and a small building, making anything but Stronghold very difficult to play. The building has several windows from which you can shoot at enemies as they cross the open ground.

Mint

The Mint provides a real challenge for just about any game type. The see-through floor in the pressing room is great for ambushing other players. Their heartbeat sensors can't detect you in the other level. There are several choke point kill zones on this map, as well.

Ship

The Ship's numerous narrow corridors and small rooms make it a good choice for any game type. The passage to the engine room on the lowest level is a kill zone. Be very careful there. If you must descend the ladder, jump down rather than climb or you're dead if an enemy waits at the bottom. Also, there's only one stairway between the ship's main levels. Keep these covered and you can make life difficult for the enemy.

Estate

Although the house is small, it has a number of rooms and three staircases. It's useful for most game types.

Skyscraper

The Skyscraper map combines large open areas with long corridors and small rooms. Use it for any type of game.

Road Ambush

Most combat on this map will take place at long range. There are several places where players can climb above ground level and shoot down on opponents. Crouch when you're in these positions to present a smaller target. Also, the long ranges make sensor detection difficult.

Amazon Research Outpost

This is an especially good map for Double Bluff or Double Stronghold games. You can exit each building unseen from the other. The open area between the two buildings can be a kill zone, however. Don't forget that you can walk on the cover over the walkway between the buildings.

Athlete's Village

This is another great map for all types of games. The ground floor is a maze of halls and rooms, and the narrow tunnels in the sewers below provide a way to sneak up behind enemies.

BioDome

BioDome is the king of maps, appropriate for any game type. There are several places to establish kill zones. If you're defending a security post, place your operatives up the stairs on the landings, where enemy heartbeat sensors can't detect you. The more players for this map, the better the game. Again, the automatic doors make sneaking up to breach difficult.

Tom Clancy's
RAINBOW SIX

MISSION PACK: EAGLE WATCH

PART 2

CHAPTER EIGHT

ADDITIONS TO THE RAINBOW TEAM

Not only does the *Eagle Watch Mission Pack* add five new missions to *Rainbow Six*, it also gives the player four new operatives and three new weapons to use in completing these missions and for multiplay. What follows are some of those additions.

New Operatives

Eagle Watch provides four new operatives to add to your teams, all taken from Tom Clancy's *Rainbow Six* novel. If you've read this great book, the names will be very familiar to you. All the new operatives are good choices for a variety of tasks.

Johnston, Homer

Personal Information

Identification Number: RCT0047-B0381
Nationality: American
Specialty: Assault
Date of Birth: 23 August 1972
Height: 183 cm
Weight: 73 kg
Hair: Blond
Eyes: Brown
Gender: Male

Background

Born in Boise, Idaho, USA. Father logger, mother secretary at lumber mill. Brought up in true mountain-man fashion. Shot his first deer at age 10. Former Green Beret and Delta Force member. Part of 101st AirMobile, Fort Campbell, Kentucky. Found his way into Black Ops by 1989. Definitive distance runner. Relies on stealth and speed to set up his sniper locations. Expert with all rifle types. Spends free time hunting with Weber and visiting his parents. Unmarried.

Notes

Johnston is one of the snipers assigned to the RAINBOW team. As such, he has great Firearms and Stealth skill levels. With the HK G3A3 rifle, he's deadly at long range. Assign Johnston to a team that must pick off tangos from a distance. He'll give you a new understanding of the sniper motto, "One shot, one kill."

Attributes

Aggression: 89
Leadership: 83
Self-control: 87
Stamina: 98
Teamwork: 88
Demolitions: 55
Electronics: 50
Firearms: 98
Grenades: 70

Loiselle, Louis

Personal Information

Identification Number: RCT0013-B5928
Nationality: French
Specialty: Assault
Date of Birth: 06 June 1968
Height: 178 cm
Weight: 68 kg
Hair: Black
Eyes: Brown
Gender: Male

Attributes

Aggression: 90
Leadership: 85
Self-control: 100
Stamina: 85
Teamwork: 89
Demolitions: 49
Electronics: 70
Firearms: 94
Grenades: 70
Stealth: 78

Background

Born in Paris, France. Married to Elaine, three years. Father former commercial pilot, mother a clerk at local department store in Avagion. Former member, French Parachute Division. Detailed to DGSE. Part of action group Service 7. Involved in tactical espionage and counterespionage throughout Europe. Began training DGSE recruits in 1985. On assignments, he's a utility player and doesn't disturb easily. He's a marksman with pistols and rifles, but is experienced in all forms of counterterrorism. He spends most free time reading and with his wife.

Notes

Loiselle is a good choice for an assault team in the support role. He'll do a great job covering your back during a mission, and will stay calm, even when stuff begins hitting the fan. Place him in a team's second slot.

Price, Eddie

Personal Information

Identification Number: RCT0049-B4197
Nationality: British
Specialty: Assault
Date of Birth: 21 September 1958
Height: 186 cm
Weight: 84 kg
Hair: Brown
Eyes: Green
Gender: Male

Background

Born in London, England. Father deceased, mother living in Cambridge, retired nurse. Price is a former color sergeant, serving in the 22nd SAS at Hereford. Spot-promoted to Sergeant Major. Spent time in Northern Ireland for the 14th Intelligence Company. Highly trained in techniques including CQB, IR photography, and covert surveillance, "the Company" performs in Northern Ireland, monitoring known IRA terrorists and preemptively striking terrorist targets. Involved in hostage rescue, Colombia, 1984. Extremely physically fit and an expert marksman. Enjoys reading, smoking his pipe, and working out with Weber. Unmarried.

Notes

Price is the first sergeant of Chavez's team in the novel. With more experience than any of the other operatives, Price makes a great team leader. Not only does he have great leadership skills, but he's also very proficient with firearms.

Attributes

Aggression: 80
Leadership: 95
Self-control: 90
Stamina: 87
Teamwork: 96
Demolitions: 71
Electronics: 63
Firearms: 96
Grenades: 77
Stealth: 89

Weber, Dieter

Personal Information

Identification Number: RCT0017-B7682
Nationality: German
Specialty: Assault
Date of Birth: 09 July 1971
Height: 191 cm
Weight: 98 kg
Hair: Blond
Eyes: Brown
Gender: Male

Attributes

Aggression: 93
Leadership: 73
Self-control: 84
Stamina: 100
Teamwork: 90
Demolitions: 53
Electronics: 61
Firearms: 100
Grenades: 72
Stealth: 96

Background

Born in Munich, Germany. Father ironworker, mother deceased. Graduate of German Army's *Berger Fuhrer* (Mountain Leader) schools, one of the world's toughest, physically. Came from GSG-9 team, part of the former Border Guards, the Federal Republic's counterterrorism team. Fluent in English and German, his marksmanship is matched by only a few team members. Spends free time hunting, working out with Price, and practicing tai kwon do. Unmarried.

Notes

Weber is another one of RAINBOW's snipers. While he has great Firearms and Stealth skill levels, he's not the best leader. You may want to control him, however, so either put him in charge of a small team or keep him alone at a distance from the action to supply fire support.

New Weapons

You now have three new weapons to use in your war against terrorism. Each of these will add more firepower to your teams and give you an advantage over your enemies.

Heckler & Koch G3A3

The G3A3 is Heckler & Koch's standard assault rifle. It fires the powerful 7.62mm NATO round. This is the most accurate rifle in RAINBOW's arsenal.

Notes

This is your best weapon choice for long-range shooting. Give this to snipers like Johnston and Weber and they'll drop tangos before the bad guys know what hit them. Sniper view has a great zoom-in and allows you to fire single rounds into the heads of tangos, even when they're near hostages.

Heckler & Koch G36K

The G36K is Heckler & Koch's latest assault rifle. Its compact design makes it useful in close quarters, and its 5.56mm round will penetrate most body armor.

Notes

Firing the same round as the M-16, the G36K gives added punch to assault teams working at short range with little room to maneuver. Use this against tangos wearing body armor when you must advance through narrow corridors or other such areas.

IMI .50 Desert Eagle

The IMI .50 Desert Eagle is a very powerful hand gun capable of punching through body armor. It has a limited six-round magazine, however.

Notes

Although the Desert Eagle has only a six-round magazine, given the limited use a secondary firearm gets, this shouldn't be a problem. Besides, with a .50-caliber round, it takes only a single shot to drop your target, even if you don't hit the tango in the head. Unless you must stay quiet, take one of these pistols along. If you must resort to your secondary weapon, this is one you can count on.

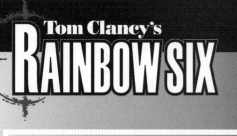

CHAPTER NINE
EAGLE WATCH MISSIONS

The five new missions included in the Eagle Watch Mission Pack can be difficult. They continue right where the original game ended, with no easy mission to help you get back into the hostage rescue business. As in Chapter 6, this chapter covers the strategies and tactics necessary to complete each of the five new missions.

The strategies include which operatives to use, how to assign them to teams, and which weapons they should carry. A brief walkthrough is then provided for each of the teams and finally, a note section describes how all the teams' individual actions should be coordinated. While you may be used to giving teams their orders and having them automatically carried out, some of the new missions will require you to take control of each of the teams at critical and hazardous instances. Therefore, be sure to include several Go codes for each team to provide pauses in the action to ease your jump from team to team.

One of the new features of the Eagle Watch Mission Pack is the Full Watch Mode. This allows the player to view the actions of all the teams during a mission, without taking control of any of them. This is a good way to test your plans for a mission and see where changes can be made as well as when your skills as a leader will be most needed during the action.

Mission 1—Operation: Little Wing

03.10.01   0600
Russia

Mission Orders

Militant terrorists have taken the Shuttle Buran site. They hold a scientist and two workers hostage, along with a bomb, in the shuttle cockpit. You must enter by way of the launch pad. Find the hostages and neutralize all terrorists at the site.

The height of the tower prevents us from providing outside heartbeat sensor support. Consider taking along a portable unit.

Objective

1. **Rescue the workers.**

Mission Data

Difficulty Level	Terrorists	Hostages	Other
Recruit	13	3	None
Veteran	18	3	None
Elite	21	3	None

Fig. 9-1. Tangos hold the workers hostage in the command section of the shuttle.

Team Assignments

Blue Team

Operative	Primary	Secondary	Slot 1	Slot 2	Uniform
Bogart	G3A3	Desert Eagle	Frag Grenade	Flashbang	Urban Light
Filatov	MP5-A2	.45 Mark 23	Heartbeat Sensor	Flashbang	Urban Light

Red Team

Operative	Primary	Secondary	Slot 1	Slot 2	Uniform
Johnston	G3A3	Desert Eagle	Frag Grenade	Flashbang	Urban Light
Rakuzanka	MP5-A2	.45 Mark 23	Heartbeat Sensor	Flashbang	Urban Light

Green Team

Operative	Primary	Secondary	Slot 1	Slot 2	Uniform
Price	G3A3	Desert Eagle	Frag Grenade	Flashbang	Urban Light
Raymond	MP5-A2	.45 Mark 23	Heartbeat Sensor	Flashbang	Urban Light

Legend

T	Terrorist
H	Hostage
⌐	Ladder Up
⌐	Ladder Down
1	Stairway Reference
△	Locked Door
/	Unlocked Door
1-A	Room Designation (first floor, first room)
▨	Stream

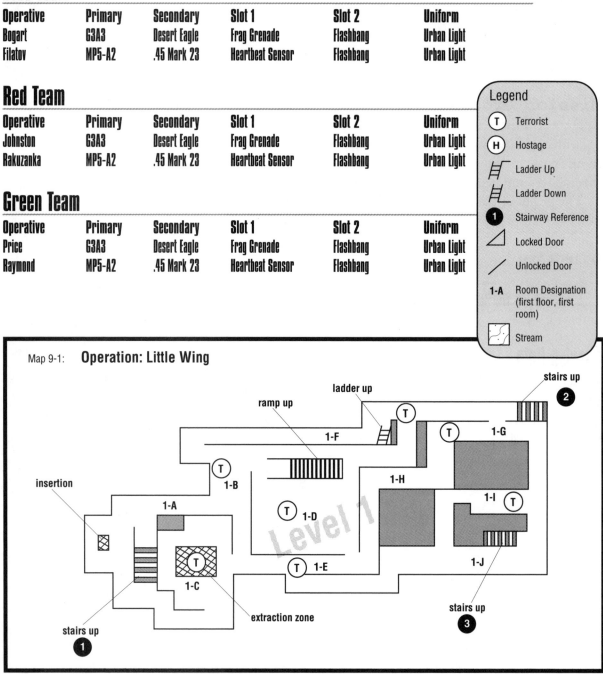

Map 9-1: **Operation: Little Wing**

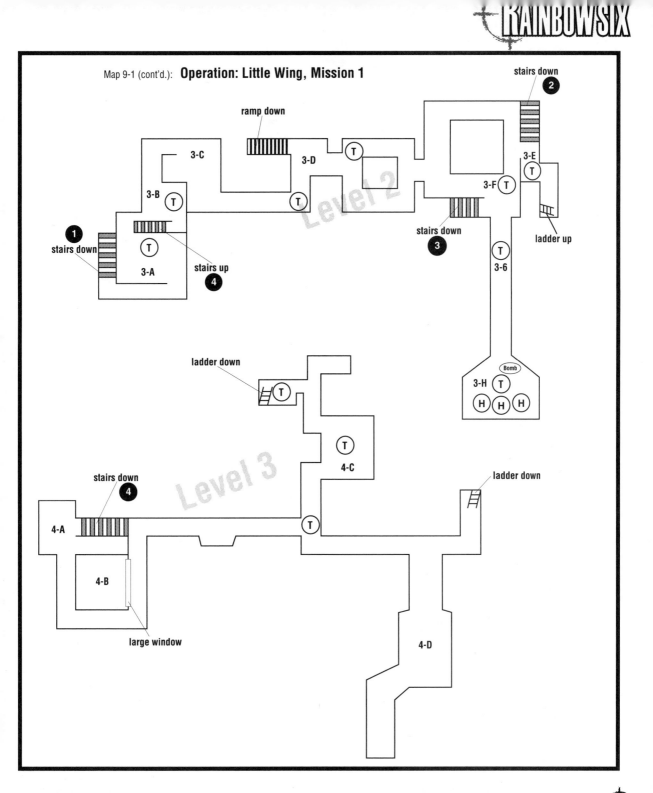

Map 9-1 (cont'd.): **Operation: Little Wing, Mission 1**

Strategy

If you thought the first mission would be just a refresher course, guess again. These tangos also have itchy trigger fingers, so you'll have to shoot fast and accurately if you're to accomplish the mission objectives without losing your entire team. Heartbeat sensors are mandatory for each team. These gadgets will help keep your operatives from being blown away as they go around a corner.

The metal walkways will make noise if you move too fast or are wearing heavy uniforms. Move quietly to avoid alerting the enemy.

You'll use three teams for this mission. It could be accomplished with only two, but that would necessitate backtracking. All three teams must advance toward the shuttle, taking out all tangos along the way. By the time they reach the shuttle, the only tango left should be the one guarding the hostages. He's very difficult to kill without endangering the hostages.

Blue Team

Blue Team is your main team. Begin by climbing the stairs near the insertion zone. Set the Rules of Engagement to Advance so your supporting operative will use the Heartbeat sensor. The first tango is in room 3-A. Throw a frag grenade around the corner to take him out. Head through the room to 3-B. Use caution as you enter here. A tango may be on the ground or up the stairs on landing 4-A. You may have to shoot up through the stairs to get him. Otherwise, he'll be in control room 4-B. If so, take him out with a grenade.

First, shoot out the glass in this room—and stay near the door. Use Sniper view to target the tango on the walkway to the shuttle. Move forward cautiously, and you can also snipe three other tangos left of this walkway. When all is clear, shoot out the shuttle windows. Hold here for Go code Alpha.

Fig. 9-2. Clear out control room 4-B, and then use it as a sniper post.

When you return to Blue Team, head out along the catwalk toward room 4-C. Throw a frag grenade into the room to take out the tango then hold again for code Alpha.

By now, you've eliminated all tangos but one. Mustering all the stealth you can, move carefully along the catwalks and across the roof of the walkway to the shuttle. Set your rifle to single-shot. Advance quietly until you can see the tango guarding the hostages through the shuttle window. Quickly take him down before he kills any hostages. If the mission doesn't end, return to the extraction zone, at code Delta, via the fourth-level walkway and stairway 4.

Red Team

Red Team's job is to clear the far side of the launch platform, as well as the area leading to the shuttle. Hold in hallway 1-A for code Bravo; then enter 1-B. There may be a tango there, so check the heartbeat sensor first. Carefully strafe left as you face area 1-D. There's a tango on your level, and a couple on the walkways above. Take out as many as you can, and then turn around and head out to the catwalk to 1-F. There's a tango at the top of the ladder in front of you and another on the catwalk at your level. Drop them both, and then head to 1-G. Clear out hallways 1-H and 1-I. Hold at the foot of stairway 2.

After another code Bravo, ascend the stairs carefully. Often you'll find a tango at the top, near 3-E. If not, wait until one appears and kill him. Then eliminate any tangos in the 3-F area, without exposing yourself to the terrorist in the shuttle at 3-H. Hold for another code Bravo.

If Blue Team can't get the tango in the shuttle, it's up to Red Team. Set your rifle to single-shot. Move forward toward the shuttle walkway. As you

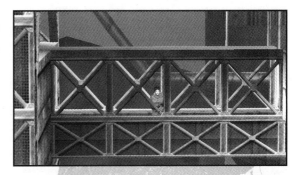
Fig. 9-3. After shooting out the control room's glass windows, take out the tango in the walkway to the shuttle.

Fig. 9-4. Blue Team must carefully and quietly walk across the roof of the walkway to the shuttle.

Fig. 9-5. Shoot through the shuttle windows to kill the tango guarding the hostages.

Fig. 9-6. Red Team must take out the tango at the top of the ladder, as well as the one on the catwalk at the same level.

Fig. 9-7. If you wait outside hallway 1-G, a tango will walk by eventually. Drop him.

Fig. 9-8. If Red Team must take out the guard, first throw a flashbang into the shuttle, and then shoot carefully down the passageway with the rifle set to single-shot.

face it, strafe a bit to the right until you can see the first two hostages, but not the tango guarding them. Throw a flashbang as far as you can into the shuttle. Then quickly choose Sniper view for the rifle and strafe right, until you see the tango. Pause briefly until the targeting reticle shrinks back down, and then fire a single round into the tango's head. Use care: even a three-round burst at this range could spread enough to kill a hostage.

With the shuttle clear, give code Delta, enter the shuttle, and then escort the hostages down stairway 3, and then to the extraction zone.

Green Team

Green Team's job is to clear an escape route for Blue Team and the hostages, should one become necessary.

Hold at the insertion zone for code Charlie. After receiving the code, take the right passage toward room 1-C. There could be a tango inside. He may not show up, because the red dot on the heartbeat sensor may be over the red line for the extraction zone. Frag the room, or at least throw a flashbang in before you enter. Hold in this room while covering hallway 1-E.

At the next code Charlie, advance toward 1-J. Then carefully climb stairway 3. Hold at the top, without exiting the stairway. You may have to help Blue Team take out a tango. At code Delta, Green Team retraces its path room 1-C and the extraction zone, clearing the path for Blue Team and the hostages.

Notes

Take control of all the teams as they encounter the enemy. While Red and Green hold near the insertion zone, take Blue Team to its first hold.

Then take command of Green Team until its next hold, followed by Red Team. Blue Team clears out 4-C, and then holds. Then Red Team climbs the stairs and waits at 3-E. Once Green Team is in the stairway, give Blue Team code Alpha to take out the guard. After the shuttle is clear, give code Delta and extract the hostages, as well as your team.

Mission 2—Operation: Sapphire Rising

03.19.01   1800
India

Mission Orders

Sikh terrorists have planted a bomb in the Taj Mahal. They also hold four hostages on the second floor. Find the bomb and disarm it, and release the hostages unharmed.

You'll be inserted on the roof of the structure. Meet back on the roof with the hostages at the extraction point.

We have set up heartbeat sensors around the Taj Mahal, so you should have full information on terrorist locations once you've been inserted.

Objectives

1. Disarm the bomb.
2. Rescue the tourists.

Fig. 9-9. Green Team must clear out the extraction zone that's also the cosmonaut suit room.

Fig. 9-10. The Taj Mahal is filled with priceless artifacts. You must free the hostages and disarm the bomb without wrecking the place.

Mission Data

Difficulty Level	Terrorists	Hostages	Other
Recruit	15	4	1 Bomb
Veteran	20	4	1 Bomb
Elite	26	4	1 Bomb

Team Assignments

Blue Team

Operative	Primary	Secondary	Slot 1	Slot 2	Uniform
Chavez	MP5SD5	.45 Mark-SD	Flashbang	Empty	Urban Medium
Yacoby	MP5SD5	.45 Mark-SD	Flashbang	Empty	Urban Medium
Morris	MP5SD5	.45 Mark-SD	Flashbang	Demolitions Kit	Urban Medium

Red Team

Operative	Primary	Secondary	Slot 1	Slot 2	Uniform
Walther	MP5SD5	.45 Mark-SD	Flashbang	Empty	Urban Medium
Loiselle	MP5SD5	.45 Mark-SD	Flashbang	Empty	Urban Medium

Green Team

Operative	Primary	Secondary	Slot 1	Slot 2	Uniform
Noronha	MP5SD5	.45 Mark-SD	Flashbang	Empty	Urban Medium
Arnavisca	MP5SD5	.45 Mark-SD	Flashbang	Empty	Urban Medium

Strategy

This is another tough mission, but it's not as bad as the first. Heartbeat sensors have been placed all around the building, so the teams needn't carry them. This gives you a big advantage, because you can see where all the tangos are hiding.

Although you can accomplish this mission with only two teams, three is best. While two teams rescue the hostages, the third goes after and disarms the bomb. Because the Taj Mahal is a historical site containing many precious artifacts, use no frag grenades and keep your shots on target. Stay as quiet as you can. If the tangos guarding the hostages see you, they'll gun down the tourists immediately.

Fig. 9-11. Blue Team must clear the roof over the enemies and prevent them from running downstairs to warn the others.

Blue Team

Blue Team's mission is to get down to the first floor and disarm the bomb. First they must clear the roof, however. From the insertion zone, head into

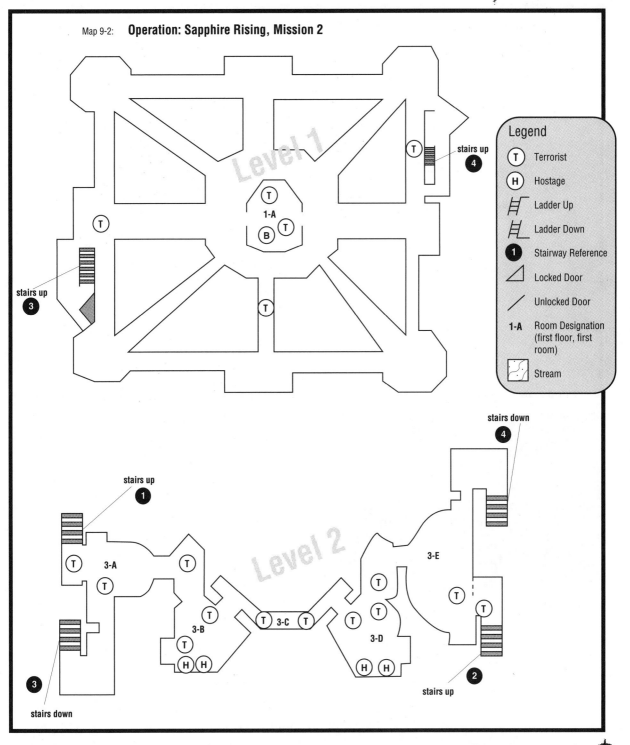

Map 9-2: **Operation: Sapphire Rising, Mission 2**

Legend

T Terrorist

H Hostage

Ladder Up

Ladder Down

1 Stairway Reference

Locked Door

Unlocked Door

1-A Room Designation (first floor, first room)

Stream

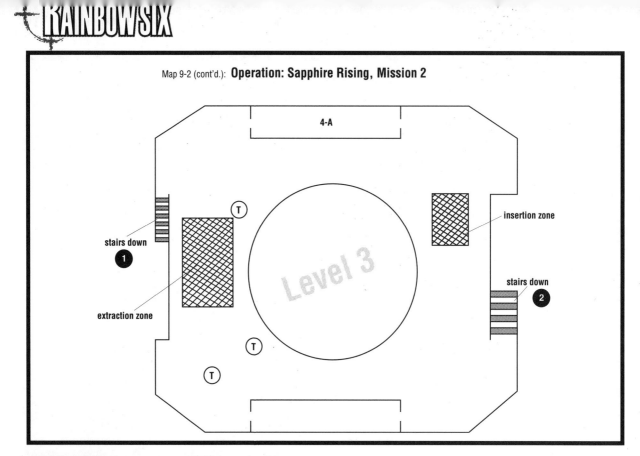

Map 9-2 (cont'd.): **Operation: Sapphire Rising, Mission 2**

4-A

stairs down
1

extraction zone

insertion zone

Level 3

stairs down
2

Fig. 9-12. Use caution as you descend the stairs.

the covered hall at 4-A, and then advance to the other end. From there, you should be able to take out at least two of the three tangos on the roof. If one tango heads toward the insertion zone, the other teams will take care of him. However, you must make sure none of them runs down stairway 1 to warn the other tangos.

With the roof clear, carefully make your way down stairway 1. There may be a tango there, or one may walk in. Clear out area 3-A, and then head to stairway 3. Hold before descending to the first floor.

At code Alpha, make your way to the ground floor. Take out any tangos in the stairway and in the hallways below. Two tangos wait in the tomb area in the center, with the bomb. Red Team should have taken them out already. If not, lob a flashbang in, and then rush it. Order Morris to disarm the bomb, and then make your way back to the roof following the path you took down.

Red Team

Red Team must rescue two of the hostages and help clear the tomb area for Blue Team.

Hold at the insertion zone for code Bravo. Take out any tangos on the roof that may have gotten away from Blue Team. Then head down stairway 2, alert for patrolling tangos. You'll probably encounter a couple of tangos in area 3-E, but you can dispatch them easily. However, area 3-D can have up to three tangos. Check the map to locate them. Throw a flashbang into the room with the tangos to stun them, and then rush in and kill them all—but don't hit the hostages.

With this area clear, move toward the balcony at 3-C and take out the two tangos there. The balcony gives you a great shot down into the tomb area. Take out both tangos in area 1-A and any others you can see. Then return to 3-D and escort the hostages back up to the roof and the extraction zone via stairway 2.

Green Team

Green Team's assignment is similar to Red's. Hold at the insertion zone until you receive code Charlie. Then follow Blue Team down stairway 1 to area 3-A. From there, look at the map to locate the hostages and tango guards in area 3-B. Take out the tango near the doorway, and then throw a flashbang into the room with the other two. Rush in and drop the stunned tangos before they can react. Finally, escort the hostages to the roof via stairway 1.

Notes

Often you can let the computer handle Red and Green teams, but the AI usually gets your men

Fig. 9-13. The tomb area holds two tangos.

Fig. 9-14. Let the demolitions expert disarm the bomb.

Fig. 9-15. Take out the two tangos on the balcony.

Fig. 9-16. From the balcony, you can take out the two tangos in the tomb area below.

Fig. 9-17. Slowly strafing to one side brings a tango into view, and you can eliminate him before he even knows you're there.

Fig. 9-18. Once the guards are dead, escort the hostages to the extraction zone on the roof.

killed, especially in the stairways. Instead, start off in control of Blue Team and clear the roof while the other two teams hold. Take Blue Team down stairway 1, and then hold at stairway 3.

Now take control of Red Team and lead them to free two of the hostages; clear the balcony as well as the tomb area below. The computer can take Red Team and the hostages back to the roof while you take control of Green Team. Get the last two hostages, and let the computer escort them to the roof. Finally, resume control of Blue Team to disarm the bomb on the ground floor and eliminate any remaining tangos.

Mission 3—Operation: Lion's Den

03.26.01   **1500**
London

Mission Orders

NOMAR terrorists have seized Parliament dignitaries and are holding them hostage in the Big Ben clock tower. Police have sealed the area around the houses. Numerous terrorists guard the tower entrance. Take out all resistance and rescue the hostages.

We've set up heartbeat sensors around the building, so you should have full information on terrorist locations once you've been inserted.

Objective

1. Rescue the dignitaries

Mission Data

Difficulty Level	Terrorists	Hostages	Other
Recruit	24	2	None
Veteran	24	2	None
Elite	26	2	None

Fig. 9-19. Terrorists have taken control of the British Parliament building and hold hostages in Big Ben's clock tower.

Team Assignments

Blue Team

Operative	Primary	Secondary	Slot 1	Slot 2	Uniform
Chavez	G3A3	Desert Eagle	Frag Grenade	Frag Grenade	Urban Medium
Arnavisca	G36K	Desert Eagle	Frag Grenade	Frag Grenade	Urban Medium
Yacoby	G36K	Desert Eagle	Frag Grenade	Frag Grenade	Urban Medium

Red Team

Operative	Primary	Secondary	Slot 1	Slot 2	Uniform
Price	G3A3	Desert Eagle	Frag Grenade	Frag Grenade	Urban Medium
Loiselle	G36K	Desert Eagle	Frag Grenade	Frag Grenade	Urban Medium
Rakuzanka	G36K	Desert Eagle	Frag Grenade	Frag Grenade	Urban Medium

Note

The tangos move about the building constantly, especially on the ground floor. Therefore, the map shows no tango locations. Use the in-game map to locate enemy positions using the heartbeat sensors set up outside the building.

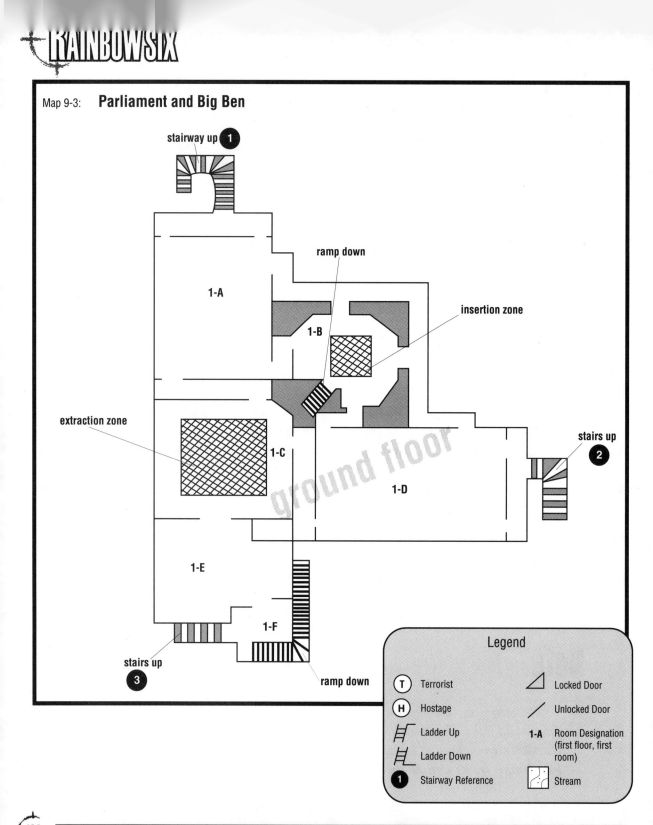

Map 9-3: **Parliament and Big Ben**

stairway up **1**

ramp down

insertion zone

1-A

1-B

extraction zone

1-C

ground floor

stairs up **2**

1-D

1-E

1-F

stairs up

3

ramp down

Legend

T Terrorist		Locked Door	
H Hostage		Unlocked Door	
Ladder Up		**1-A**	Room Designation (first floor, first room)
Ladder Down			
1 Stairway Reference			Stream

Strategy

This is a tough mission. Right from the beginning, tangos will come after you and your teams. All the tangos wear body armor, so take along weapons that will penetrate.

You begin on the ground floor of Parliament. You'll need two teams for this mission. While one secures the ground floor, the other heads up the clock tower to rescue the hostages.

Heartbeat sensors already have been placed around the building, so your teams needn't carry them. You'll find most tangos waiting around corners. A great tactic for getting through this mission is to bounce a frag grenade off an opposite wall back toward the target.

Fig. 9-20. Blue Team heads down into the tunnel, where it will wait for the ground floor to be cleared.

Blue Team

Blue is the hostage rescue team. From the start, have them run down into the tunnel under Parliament and hold halfway through it.

At code Alpha, continue down the tunnel and emerge at area 1-F. The ground floor should be clear by now. One or two tangos wait on stairway 3's first landing. Take them out, and then make your way up the clock tower. At each corner, check your map to see what lies ahead. At least one tango awaits you on each flight. Frag grenades work well for taking them out without exposing yourself. Also, strafe slowly past the corner until you can just barely see the enemy. Switch to Sniper view and inch out just a bit more so you can shoot them quickly in the body or head.

After several flights, you will come to a large room with gears. To the right of the door are two or three tangos. Bounce a frag grenade off the gears and you can take them all out with a single blast. Clear out this room and then head up the next flight of stairs, which lead to the last room.

Fig. 9-21. At code Alpha, emerge from the tunnel.

Fig. 9-22. Strafe slowly past stairway corners until you can just see tangos ahead. Shoot them before they can see and fire at you.

Fig. 9-23. Pick off the tangos from below, before they can harm the hostages they're guarding.

Fig. 9-24. When the area is secure, escort the hostages to safety. One looks like the Belgian ambassador to Great Britain.

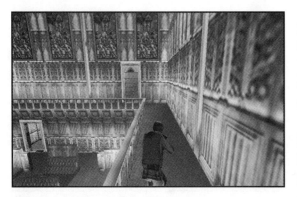

Fig. 9-25. Secure the House of Commons, and then head up to the overhead walkway.

Set your team's ROE to Clear. Carefully make your way into the room. There are several terrorists in this room and two on the walkway above, with the hostages. Move counterclockwise along the wall as you take out the tangos on your level. Try to pick off the tangos overhead, as well.

You must clear this area quickly, before the tangos can kill the hostages. When the area is secure, escort the dignitaries down the clock tower to the extraction zone in room 1-C.

Red Team

It's Red Team's job to secure the ground floor. At the start of the mission, expect at least one tango to come and check out the insertion zone. Drop him, and then head into the House of Commons (1-D) and take out any tangos there. Next, head up stairway 2. Watch out for tangos that may be coming down. At the top of the stairs, follow the walkway to the House of Lords (1-A).

Along the way, you'll pass two openings that look down on rooms 1-C and 1-E. From there, you can shoot down at the tangos covering the extraction zone. There may be two or three. Take out as many as you can now, so there will be fewer later.

Continue to the House of Lords, and make your way down stairway 1. Clear out this large room, and then finish off any survivors in room 1-C before securing area 1-E. Finally, hold short of stairway 3 while Blue Team rescues the hostages. At code Delta, head for the extraction zone.

Notes

It's not difficult to operate both teams during this mission. Start in control of Red Team. Secure the ground floor while the computer takes Blue Team into the safety of the tunnel to await code Alpha.

When Red Team's job is complete, take control of Blue Team and head up the clock tower to rescue the hostages. Red Team will cover the foot of the stairs to prevent missed tangos from sneaking up on Blue Team. As Blue and the hostages reach the ground floor, give code Delta so Red Team will lead the way to the extraction zone, and the end of the mission.

Mission 4—Operation: Red Lightning

034.04.01   2400
China

Mission Orders

Kang revolutionaries have captured tourists visiting the fabled Forbidden City. They've divided the hostages into three groups and are holding them in separate buildings. Find the hostages and meet at center court for transport out.

We've set up heartbeat sensors all around the city, so you should have full information on terrorist locations once you've inserted.

Objective

1. Rescue the tourists.

Mission Data

Difficulty Level	Terrorists	Hostages	Other
Recruit	18	5	None
Veteran	21	5	None
Elite	28	5	None

Fig. 9-26. From the walkway, you can take out tangos below in rooms 1-C and 1-E.

Fig. 9-27. Red Team covers the stairway as Blue Team goes up for the hostages.

Fig. 9-28. Everyone made it safely to the extraction zone.

Team Assignments

Blue Team

Operative	Primary	Secondary	Slot 1	Slot 2	Uniform
Walther	MP5SD5	.45 Mark-SD	Flashbang	Empty	Urban Medium
Maldini	MP5SD5	.45 Mark-SD	Flashbang	Empty	Urban Medium

Red Team

Operative	Primary	Secondary	Slot 1	Slot 2	Uniform
Bogart	MP5SD5	.45 Mark-SD	Flashbang	Empty	Urban Medium
Burke	MP5SD5	.45 Mark-SD	Flashbang	Empty	Urban Medium

Green Team

Operative	Primary	Secondary	Slot 1	Slot 2	Uniform
Noronha	MP5SD5	.45 Mark-SD	Flashbang	Empty	Urban Medium
Hanley	MP5SD5	.45 Mark-SD	Flashbang	Empty	Urban Medium

Fig. 9-29. Terrorists hold five hostages within the Forbidden City.

Strategy

This mission is easier than previous ones. In fact, you can probably let the computer handle some teams for part of the mission.

Your teams begin outside the Forbidden City. They must infiltrate as quietly as possible and rescue the five tourists held hostage on the second floor of three different buildings. Heartbeat sensors are positioned all around the compound, so your teams needn't carry them. The plan is for the three teams to clear the entire ground level before assaulting the second floors and securing the hostages.

Blue Team

Blue Team must lead the way for the other two teams and help clear out most of the ground level. From the insertion zone, carefully enter area 1-B. Take out a possible tango in area 1-A, and then another in 1-C. Then head through 1-A to the entrance to 1-F. Switch to Sniper view just before entering 1-F and look up at the second-floor balcony. Take out the tango patrolling there, followed by the one at ground level.

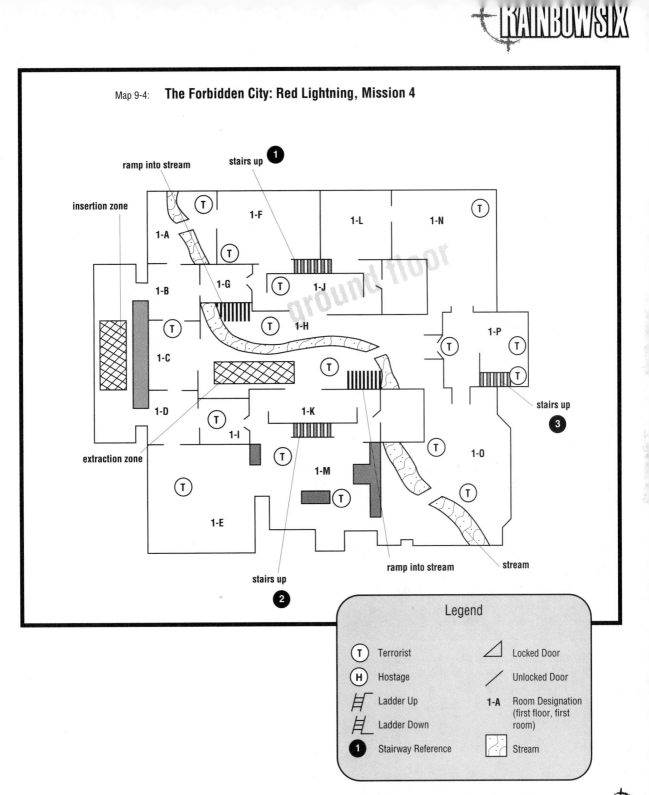

Map 9-4: **The Forbidden City: Red Lightning, Mission 4**

ground floor

ramp into stream

stairs up ❶

insertion zone

1-F

1-A

1-L

1-N

1-B

1-G

1-J

1-C

1-H

1-P

1-D

extraction zone

1-K

1-I

stairs up ❸

3

stream

1-O

1-M

1-E

ramp into stream

stairs up ❷

Legend

ⓣ	Terrorist	◹	Locked Door
Ⓗ	Hostage	⁄	Unlocked Door
⌐	Ladder Up	**1-A**	Room Designation (first floor, first room)
⌐	Ladder Down		
❶	Stairway Reference		Stream

Rush into building 1-J and clear the ground floor there, as well as courtyard 1-H. Continue to area 1-L and 1-N, where another tango patrols. From 1-N, you can take out the two tangos in building 1-P. Carefully enter the building and clear area 1-O from inside 1-P. Now move to the stairs and hold.

At code Alpha, carefully climb halfway up the stairs. Set the ROE to Clear. Then turn a little past 90 degrees to the right and throw a flashbang over the railing into the upstairs room. Quickly switch back to your rifle and rush up the stairs to take out the stunned tango. Locate the hostage and escort her to the stairway. Hold for code Delta, and then take the hostage to the extraction zone.

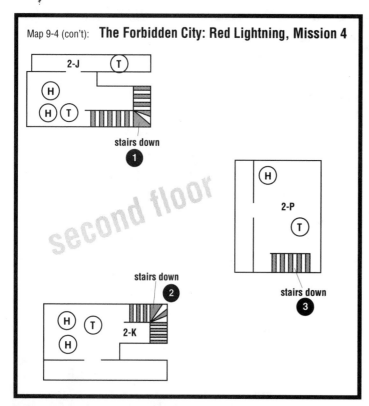

Fig. 9-30. Blue Team carefully moves into the first area. If you're quiet, you can take out the first tango or two without them even knowing you're there.

Red Team

While Blue Team clears the northern part of the compound, Red Team will secure the southern areas.

From the beginning, move over to the wall near the opening to area 1-D and hold. At code Bravo, rush into 1-D and take out the tangos in 1-E and 1-I before you enter area 1-I. Open the door and enter building 1-K. From the doorway, clear out area 1-M, and then hold.

At code Bravo, rush halfway up the stairs. Set ROE to Clear and throw a flashbang over the railing, 40 degrees left. After it goes off, rush up and take out the tango. Locate the two hostages and escort them to the stairway before holding. At code Delta, take the hostages to the extraction zone.

Fig. 9-31. Before entering 1-F, shoot the tango up on the balcony using Sniper view.

Fig. 9-32. Be wary of a tango descending the stairs as you enter 1-F.

Fig. 9-33. Clear out the courtyard from inside building 1-J.

Fig. 9-34. Throw a flashbang over the railing before you take out the tango in room 2-P.

Fig. 9-35. A tango lies dead ahead as Red Team enters the Forbidden City. Watch for the tango in area 1-E, as well.

Fig. 9-36. Take out the two tangos in area 1-M before holding at the stairway.

Fig. 9-37. Throw a flashbang over the railing to stun the tango before rushing up to the second floor and rescuing the hostages.

Fig. 9-38. Green Team rescues the two hostages in room 2-J.

Fig. 9-39. The three teams take the hostages to the courtyard extraction zone.

Green Team

Green Team will face only one tango, because Blue Team has cleared its path already. Hold at the insertion zone for code Charlie. Then go through 1-B and 1-G into building 1-J. Hold at the stairway. At code Charlie, set the ROE to Clear, move halfway up, and throw a flashbang about 40 degrees right, over the railing. After it goes off, rush up the stairs and kill the tango. Escort the two hostages to the stairway and hold for Code Delta. Finally, take the hostages to the extraction zone.

Notes

You should begin in control of Blue Team. Clear out the areas along your path. Usually, you can give Red and Green teams codes Bravo and Charlie, respectively, after you clear courtyard 1-H.

The computer has no trouble with Green Team, but Red Team can run into trouble taking out the two tangos in area 1-M. You may want to control them through this area. All teams will hold at the stairways. It doesn't matter which goes first, but you should control their assaults to rescue the hostages. When all hostages have been rescued, give code Delta to return all teams to the extraction zone.

Mission 5—Operation: Eagle Watch

04.13.01   0900
Washington, D.C.

Mission Orders

Members of the Red Sun Brigade posed as tourists to get past security at the capitol building. Inside, they killed a security officer and secured hostages—along with a cache of weapons. Police managed to clear the building and have blocked off exits. Recon tells us there's a bomb in the building, controlled by a terrorist via remote. Defuse the bomb before you approach the Senate chamber, or the tango will set it off.

Fig. 9-40. Terrorists have planted a bomb in the U.S. capitol building and hold a Senator and an aide hostage.

We've set up heartbeat sensors around the capitol building, so you should have full information on terrorist locations once you've inserted.

Objectives

1. Prevent bomb detonation.
2. Rescue both hostages.

Mission Data

Difficulty Level	Terrorists	Hostages	Other
Recruit	25	2	1 Bomb
Veteran	25	2	1 Bomb
Elite	25	2	1 Bomb

Team Assignments

Blue Team

Operative	Primary	Secondary	Slot 1	Slot 2	Uniform
Chavez	MP5SD5	.45 Mark-SD	Frag Grenade	Flashbang	Urban Medium
Johnston	MP5SD5	.45 Mark-SD	Frag Grenade	Flashbang	Urban Medium
Yacoby	MP5SD5	.45 Mark-SD	Frag Grenade	Flashbang	Urban Medium

Red Team

Operative	Primary	Secondary	Slot 1	Slot 2	Uniform
Price	MP5SD5	.45 Mark-SD	Frag Grenade	Flashbang	Urban Medium
Weber	MP5SD5	.45 Mark-SD	Frag Grenade	Flashbang	Urban Medium
Raymond	MP5SD5	.45 Mark-SD	Frag Grenade	Flashbang	Urban Medium

Green Team

Operative	Primary	Secondary	Slot 1	Slot 2	Uniform
Walther	MP5SD5	.45 Mark-SD	Frag Grenade	Flashbang	Urban Medium
McAllen	MP5SD5	.45 Mark-SD	Frag Grenade	Demolitions Kit	Urban Medium

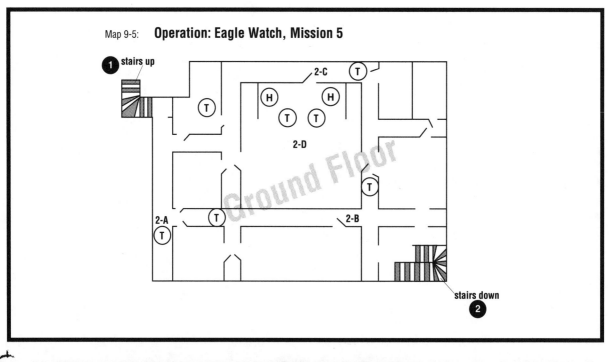

Map 9-5: **Operation: Eagle Watch, Mission 5**

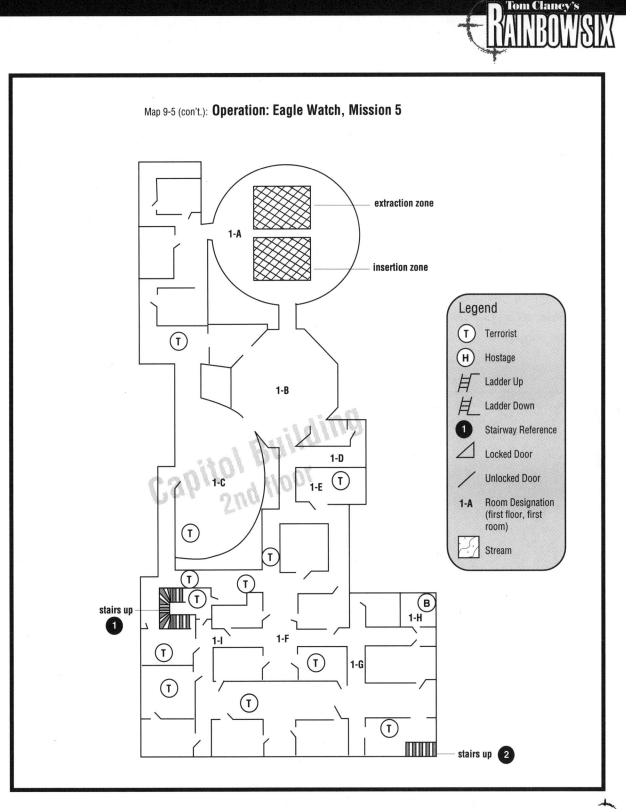

Map 9-5 (con't.): **Operation: Eagle Watch, Mission 5**

extraction zone

insertion zone

1-A

T

1-B

1-D

1-C

1-E   T

T

T

T

T

T

stairs up

1   1-I   1-F

T   B   1-H

T   1-G

T   T

T

T

stairs up   2

Legend

T   Terrorist

H   Hostage

Ladder Up

Ladder Down

1   Stairway Reference

Locked Door

Unlocked Door

1-A   Room Designation
(first floor, first
room)

Stream

Capitol Building
2nd floor

Tip

Give your teams the Clear order as they enter a room or a hallway where you expect some resistance. This keeps computer-controlled operatives ready to kill tangos in surrounding areas, as well as along the waypoints.

Fig. 9-41. Blue Team takes the lead and clears the hallways of the first floor.

Strategy

This can be a difficult mission, but you don't have to do it alone. Just control Blue Team, and the computer can take care of the rest.

This mission's objectives are twofold. First, disarm a bomb on the ground floor. Then rescue two hostages held in the senate chamber on the second floor. One team goes after the hostages, another disarms the bomb, and the third provides support for the first two. Heartbeat sensors have been placed all around the building, so your teams needn't carry this item.

Blue Team

You should control Blue Team. Although its main task is to rescue the hostages, it also will help clear the ground floor of tangos. From the insertion zone, head through 1-B to 1-F, and then hold at 1-G. You'll have to kill several tangos along the way, but as long as you stay quiet, no one will come looking for you.

At code Alpha, after the bomb has been disarmed, head up stairway 2. A tango guards the foot of the stairs, so take him out before rushing in.

At the top of the stairs, make sure no tangos wait to ambush you, and then head to 2-C. Open the door while standing to one side and take out the two tangos on your level, as well as others in the balcony above. Two or three tangos wait on the balcony above the door, as well. Face the door and look up; then slowly walk backward until you can throw a frag grenade onto the balcony and kill them all.

With the chamber clear, escort the hostages out and down stairway 2. Continue to the extraction zone at 1-A, following the path you took earlier. Be careful: you may encounter a tango or two on the way.

Red Team

Red Team's job is to provide support for Blue and Green teams as they perform their tasks. From the insertion zone, rush into

area 1-B and hold near the doorway into chamber 1-C. A couple tangos wait in this room.

At code Bravo, rush down to 1-I and cover the hallways while Green Team disarms the bomb. Following the next code Bravo, rush up stairway 1 to the second floor and proceed to 2-A, and then 2-B. Hold at this last point and cover Blue Team's egress route after it rescues the hostages. When you receive code Delta, rush down stairway 2 and lead Blue Team back to the extraction zone, taking out any tangos along the way.

Fig. 9-44. Watch out for the tango guard at the foot of stairway 2.

Fig. 9-42. If you enter room 1-E, you'll find a library where a tango hides behind some bookshelves. Move quietly into the room and shoot him through a gap in the books.

Fig. 9-45. Open the door to the Senate chamber carefully. You must take out both the tangos on the floor and those in the balcony above.

Fig. 9-43. While Green Team takes care of the bomb, cover stairway 2. One or two tangos may walk out. Drop them before they can cause trouble.

Fig. 9-46. Red Team covers chamber 1-C while Blue Team advances down the hallways. There are tangos on the floor and up in the balcony.

Fig. 9-47. Cover the hallway while Green Team deactivates the bomb.

Fig. 9-48. Red Team rushes up stairway 1.

Fig. 9-49. Let the demolitions expert do his job. With the bomb disarmed, the mission is half completed.

Green Team

Green Team's mission—disarm the bomb—is easy. In fact, if the other two teams do their jobs, Green Team won't have to kill any tangos. From the start, move through 1-B and hold at 1-D. When you get code Charlie, head to room 1-H and disarm the bomb. With your task complete, head back to the extraction zone and wait for the mission to end.

Notes

This mission is fairly straightforward. If you command Blue Team, the computer will have no trouble taking control of Red and Green teams. Take Blue Team all the way to 1-G and cover the halls and stairs. Give codes Bravo and Charlie to send Red Team to cover 1-I and Green Team to disarm the bomb. When Green Team reports that the bomb is deactivated, give codes Alpha and Bravo.

Take Blue Team upstairs to rescue the hostages, while Red Team clears the hallways on the other side of the second floor. When the hostages are being escorted, give code Delta to send Red Team out ahead of you to cover the escape route for Blue Team and the hostages. The mission ends when the hostages arrive at the extraction zone.

Fig. 9-50. The hostages are rescued safely and escorted to the extraction zone.

Along with the five new single-player missions, which you can also play in cooperative multiplayer mode, *Eagle Watch* adds several new mission types and maps. You can use the three new weapons against other human opponents, as well. The following paragraphs cover additions to the multiplayer game.

New Adversarial Games

This mission pack gives you six new mission types from which to select adversarial games. All are great for as many players as you can get together.

Assassination

In assassination games, each team has a leader, who looks like a civilian, at its base. The object is to locate and kill the other team's leader before it kills yours. There are a couple of ways to play this mission. You could just sit back at your base and take out the enemy team as it comes after your leader, and then go after the opposing leader. Or you can leave a guard or two at the base and send the rest of your team out to hunt down and kill the other team's leader.

Scatter Assassination

This game resembles Assassination except the operatives of each team are scattered about the map instead of beginning together at the base.

Terrorist Hunt

The mission gives multiplayers an extremely competitive mixture of team survival and terrorist hunting. Each team begins at a base. Your goal is to be the first team to eliminate half the terrorists without being taking out yourselves by the opposing team. (Of course, nothings to keep you from killing the other team.) This is a good game for two or three players, because it gives each team more to shoot at.

Fig. 10-1. In Assassination games, you must kill the other team's leader—the one who looks like a civilian.

Scatter Hunt

Scatter Hunt is like Terrorist Hunt except teams begin scattered about the map rather than together at a base.

Save Your Base

In this interesting game type, each team begins at a base and must locate a detonator of corresponding color. The detonator will set off a bomb at the base unless the team can deactivate it before the other team can do the same.

Although the primary objective is to locate the detonator and shut it down, it's also a good strategy to locate the other team's detonator and guard it. The longer you can prevent the enemy from deactivating theirs, the more time your team has to find its own.

It's a good idea to designate one or two team members demolitions specialists. They should carry a demolitions kit to help them disarm the bomb quickly. The player deactivating the detonator is a sitting duck, so protect that player as he or she works.

Tip

The base where your leader is located isn't always the best place to maintain a good defense, so you may want to consider taking him someplace safer. To move your leader, choose the Escort ROE and the leader will follow you. Remember to change the ROE once he is in a safe place so you don't lead him into danger.

Fig. 10-2. In Save Your Base games, your team must locate your detonator and disarm it before the other team can deactivate their detonator.

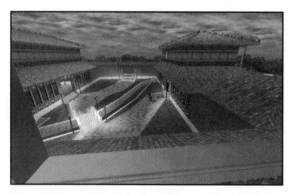

Fig. 10-3. From the balconies of the two-story buildings, you can snipe at the other teams and even throw grenades down on them.

Scattered Teams

Scattered Teams resembles Team Survival from the original game in that the objective is to kill all opposing players. However, in Scattered Team, all players start scattered about the map rather than together at their team bases.

New Maps

With the five single-player missions come five new multiplayer maps. All make for challenging games.

Shuttle Pad

This is an excellent map for all game types, especially Stronghold and Assassination games, because it provides some great areas to hole up. The combination of inside and outside areas also allows you to engage in both long-range sniping and close-quarters combat.

Taj Mahal

This large building can be a lot of fun. The many small rooms provide some close combat. The long hallways can be deathtraps if an attacker isn't careful. Because the building is a museum, there are a lot of glass cases you can shoot up for extra noise, which you can use as a diversion.

Big Ben

Big Ben makes a great multiplayer map. All the balconies—ideal for ambushes—allow for a variety of defenses. The clock tower provides one long kill zone. When playing Assassination games where the clock tower isn't a base, try to get your leader to the top for easier protection.

Forbidden City

The Forbidden City can be a challenging map. All three two-story buildings have balconies from which snipers can fire down on other teams. Take a lot of grenades to throw over walls, either from ground level or from balconies. Sometimes you can throw grenades into the other team's base from the central building's balcony.

Capitol Building

This map is ideal for any adversarial game. Its balconies, staircases, many rooms, and doorways allow for some major firefights and great ambushes. For the Capitol Building, consider taking breaching charges along to make a big entrance. Several long hallways are useful for defense. Stay far enough from corners to avoid losses to corner-tossed enemy grenades.

Maps with Terrorists

Several adversarial game types allow you to choose a map featuring terrorists. This can add a lot more adventure, especially when only a few players are participating. It's also exciting in large games, because bullets will fly everywhere. Try different types of games with terrorists, but remember to take enough ammo for all the targets.

City Street Large

This is the same area from the Fire and Movement Training exercise with underground passages and the ability to enter all of the buildings. While the area is quite small, it allows for some great ambushes and makes a quick game. Be sure to watch your back because most buildings have more than one entry.

Killhouse 2

This area builds on the two-story killhouse by adding a second and identical killhouse. Though it is a small battle area, attacks on enemy bases can be deadly if your opponent sets up a good defense. Bring along grenades for throwing around corners and set up snipers on the roofs.

Name	Specialty	Aggression	Leadership	Self-Control	Stamina	Teamwork	Demolitions	Electronics	Firearms	Grenades	Stealth
Arnavisca, Santiago	Assault	72	81	94	83	92	24	34	100	65	82
Beckenbauer, Lars	Demolitions	55	78	77	81	74	100	91	76	80	72
Bogart, Daniel	Assault	89	96	93	97	95	20	20	98	50	73
Burke, Andrew	Assault	91	85	75	94	89	75	53	93	67	78
Chavez, Ding	Assault	95	100	92	97	94	71	67	100	74	100
DuBarry, Alain	Electronics	72	81	76	91	66	76	100	84	81	73
Filatov, Genedy	Assault	82	82	87	83	88	62	36	91	85	70
Haider, Karl	Assault	100	75	71	96	93	42	55	89	71	74
Hanley, Timothy	Assault	93	86	84	100	86	75	65	91	84	85
Johnston, Homer	Assault	89	83	87	98	88	55	50	98	70	100
Lofquist, Annika	Electronics	80	92	77	82	88	61	97	85	69	69
Loiselle, Louis	Assault	90	85	100	85	89	49	70	94	70	78
Maldini, Antonio	Recon	50	60	80	95	80	65	65	90	50	100
McAllen, Roger	Demolitions	70	70	70	98	90	97	71	96	100	70
Morris, Gerald	Demolitions	40	72	80	79	89	99	54	80	97	71
Noronha, Alejandro	Assault	91	91	91	82	87	50	32	94	75	73
Price, Eddie	Assault	80	95	90	87	96	71	63	96	77	89
Rakuzanka, Kazimiera	Assault	85	85	60	96	94	50	52	96	70	80
Raymond, Renee	Assault	75	79	90	91	100	30	23	97	85	96
Sweeney, Kevin	Recon	45	65	95	85	90	30	96	90	50	99
Walther, Jorg	Assault	76	97	90	96	98	71	89	96	83	67
Weber, Dieter	Assault	93	73	84	100	90	53	61	100	72	96
Woo, Tracy	Recon	50	75	85	96	96	30	85	80	50	98
Yacoby, Ayana	Recon	95	65	70	95	75	30	86	97	60	97

INDEX

Z

[0] **key on keypad**

to manipulate environment, 2, 3

to perform special action, 57

**Zooming in and out with square
bracket keys, 2**

Coming July 1999 From Red Storm Entertainment

WARFARE FOR THE 21ST CENTURY